BEHIND
THE GOAL

Memories of Bristol City's East End

First published 2015 by DB Publishing, an imprint of JMD Media Ltd, Nottingham, United Kingdom.

ISBN 9781780914824

BEHIND THE GOAL

Memories of Bristol City's East End

Neil Palmer &
Bristol City Football Club

Contents

*This book is dedicated to my late friend Tom Garvey.
A loyal Bristol City fan. It's fitting that a book about
memories should be dedicated to a man that created so
many wonderful ones for his family and friends.*

AKNOWLEGEMENTS

I would like to take this opportunity to thank everybody connected with this project. This book could not have been written without countless peoples co-operation. I would like to thank my wife Sally, who knew when I had the idea for this book it would mean a year of me spent on the computer, travelling to meet people and relaying stories of various Bristol City footballers that quite frankly she had no idea what I was talking about. So I thank you for your patience and continued support and I will not give up in my attempt to get you interested in the game.

Ideas for books are fine but they then have to be turned into something tangible so I would like to thank DB Publishing and Steve Caron for getting the idea going along with Bristol City Football Club and notably David Lloyd, Adam Baker and Luke Palmer who have given me tremendous support and agreed that we should not let the passing of the End go unnoticed. Thanks also to DB Publishing's editor Paul Dalling for his work on my book. Thanks must also go to David Woods and Tom Hopegood who along with their excellent publications *The Bristol Babe* and *Bristol City 1894–67* answered many of my questions. I also thank Geoff Twentyman who always supports any sports project like this and three original East Enders, Angus Nutt, John 'Doddy' Dodimead and Tom Hopegood who were a pleasure to spend time with and our chats could have been a book on their own. My appreciation goes out to all the Bristol City players I interviewed notably Jantzen Derrick and Louis Carey who went beyond the call of duty regarding helping out. I have been deeply touched by the support the fans have given to the book and my biggest thank you goes to all the people who took the time to telephone, email, write letters and track me down in order to tell their story. I hope I have done them and the East End proud.

FOREWORD

I felt extremely honoured when Neil asked me to write the foreword for this book. Everybody knows how I feel about my hometown club Bristol City, yet I don't really get the chance to talk about the supporters and how important they are to a club. There are some exciting things happening at Bristol City, not only on the pitch but off it. The new stand complex will, I'm sure be amazing, yet I like many supporters want to mark the passing of the East End. It was not really much to look at yet the contribution that part of the ground made over the years should never be forgotten. I don't want supporters who have supported City from the Williams stand, Atyeo stand or the Dolman to feel that their contribution is not valued, it certainly is but with the East End being no more I just wanted to tell you how I feel about its passing.

I first stepped inside Ashton Gate as an eight-year-old. I went to see Liverpool in a pre season friendly with my dad and his John Motson sheepskin coat. We watched the 3–3 draw from the Williams stand and from that moment I was hooked on the Robins. Even at that early age I could not help myself having the occasional look to my right at the noise coming from that old stand. I remember saying to my dad 'What's that bit called? 'That's the East End' he replied.

I remember thinking that looks like fun but I didn't really know why. I continued to go to games with my dad and when I signed schoolboy forms for the club I was, along with all the other schoolboys given a free match ticket for The Dolman stand. Again I would find myself watching the game and also the East End. I would laugh at some of the songs that came resonating out of that dark hole of a place and it seemed like the singing started there and went right round the ground until it reached us in the Dolman where we would join in. I loved it when they gave a particular rival player stick and when City scored at that end they would literally go mental. I eventually found myself in there thanks to my mates and I was not disappointed. I had a great time singinging dancing and I felt like I had a real day out. I know it had a bad reputation in the 70s and early 80s but I never felt threatened in there. I cannot emphasise how important supporters are to a team. I remember playing on my home debut against Walsall the noise that I could hear in the tunnel is something that I will never forget, you have to bear in mind I had been playing schoolboy games, youth games then reserves in front of a handful of fans then suddenly here I am at Ashton Gate. There is a moment as you are in the tunnel where you first hear the fans and it sends a shiver down your spine. It only lasts for a couple of seconds but that feeling is something I experienced every time I ran out as a Bristol City player. It really is the biggest adrenalin buzz you could ever have. I think back to the season where we got beaten in the play-off Final against Hull City under Gary Johnson. I think I can honestly say that it was the best City team I ever played in. We had a never-say-die attitude and that was the same for the supporters. They never ever gave up on us they were truly the 12th man and even if we went a goal down they immediately sang our names and as a player you felt 10 feet tall and capable of anything. I am also reminded of the play-off semi-final against Hartlepool at Ashton Gate. I have never ever felt such atmosphere in my life. I could see the ground physically shaking it was a phenomenal night, that again only supporters can create, it was tribal and we felt like we could achieve anything with them behind us. Then I think of going to Hull City midweek when we were already relegated from the Championship and Hull were fighting for the play-offs. I remember being on the team bus and looking out of the coach window at the fans as we pulled into the KC stadium. I saw a young bloke with his son decked out in his red and white scarf. I thought to myself here is a guy who has taken time off from work, travelled hundreds of miles to come here and support the City even though they are already relegated. That's why we play football and fans like him are as important to this club as any player or manager will ever be.

When I look back at the East End there are obviously fans that will never understand the affection for the place by certain City fans. I have to admit I understand why the club had to put seating in the end particularly after Lord Chief Justice Taylor's report but I thought it lost atmosphere. When you go to a gig or a show with singing and dancing the one thing you want is to engage with the performance and get up out of your seat, it's a natural instinct and it's no different with football. I also feel the club made the wrong decision in putting away fans in the East End. The end held its own noise due to the roof. If we were playing in front of 12,000 with say 2,000 away fans the noise those away fans made in the East End made it seem like they had 10,000 in there, bearing in mind that most away fans are a hard-core type of supporter who have come out for a good days singing. The noise stayed in the East End then drifted around the ground. If the club had given away fans a section of the

Atyeo they would be lost as their singing would just drift off into the air due to the high roof. I am sure the powers that be at the club will take those sorts of things on board with the new structure's design. It is a new era for Bristol City and I find myself following the club as a fan. I have always understood the importance of connecting with those on the terraces, but I know that can become more and more difficult in the modern game. As a player and a captain I always made sure we as players clapped the supporters as we left the field and that was always reciprocated by the fans even though at times we did not deserve it. So I would like to take this opportunity to tell each and everyone one of them how important they were to me in my career and what a great contribution they made to our success. I look forward to reading fans stories of times spent in the East End throughout the decades and I hope the modern Bristol City will provide a host of memories for people like us. Fans.

Louis Carey

INTRODUCTION

Behind the goal tells the story of Bristol City's East End in the words of fans who have watched football from its terracing since it was rebuilt in 1928 and became the structure we know it to be today. Over the years it has taken on many names, my father refers to it as the covered end, and to my son it's the Wedlock stand. But to me and my generation of fans born in the 1960s it will always be the East End. A place that was hallowed ground to City fans and a place of fear for rival fans.

The book is really a work of oral history with recollections, opinions and impressions taken from many emails, letters, telephone conversations and interviews conducted by myself with players and fans alike since the initial idea of the book in the summer of 2014. *Behind the goal* is not meant to be a definitive history of Bristol City Football Club, it is merely a selection of fans and players memories of a place at Ashton Gate that meant so much, to so many people and the response to the project has clearly shown this to be true. Player's play manager's manage and everybody else at a football club goes about their work to do the best for the common goal. But without supporters there would be no point to football. It is the biggest sport in the world and our nations favourite game. People are prepared to pay to watch it more than any other sport in the land. It's exciting, dramatic and as it is relatively unstructured and that appeals to many different kinds of people on so many levels. Over the years the bulk of footballs audience has watched the game standing up. A place on the football terraces is culturally and economically accessible to everyone and has always given supporters a sense of participation by way of singing, chanting and creating an atmosphere that so easily gets transferred onto the pitch, many comments from players in this book will vouch for that. The terracing was not only places of entertainment but safe, environments, offering the paying customer a sense of community and a way to release emotions from the daily tedium. The importance to the people who stood on them explains why many of these ends became as famous as the clubs themselves. Terracing such as United's Stretford end, Liverpool's Kop, Villas Holte end and Chelsea's Shed end are testimony to this.

The move to all seater stadiums following the tragedies at Heysel and Hillsborough is the most significant development to date in the history of football as a spectator sport. The government realised that further legislation was necessary. The 1971 Ibrox disaster where 66 fans lost their lives and 200 were injured due to crushing after a old firm derby had brought in The Safety of Sports Act, but this had failed to solve the problems of crumbling stadiums and terracing and was anachronistic in its recommendations on crowd control. There is an argument to keep standing as fans certainly seem to like it and many are loath to see it disappear from the modern game. Yet football clubs have been put in a difficult position since Lord Justice Taylor's report which made recommendations for all Premier League and First Division grounds to be all seater by 1994. Clubs have had to not only respect the past at their grounds but also realise that they are in the entertainment industry and have to give supporters the best experience when coming to games. Many anecdotes from supporters of a certain age in these pages will highlight the unwillingness to remove standing with the phrase 'I used to go until they put the seats in'. In fact this could easily have been the title of this book. What is certain is that the experience of watching football from the terraces has been a profoundly important part of millions of people's lives for over a century. These great sweeps of concrete terracing with their enormous passionate and loyal fans, have now disappeared and been replaced with tip up seats. In this book I hope to capture through supporters memories one such piece of Bristol City's history.

Having lived in Bristol all my life I have seen many changes to this wonderful city, both good and many bad and many of those changes have gone without any sort of remembrance. So when I heard that Bristol City would be demolishing that side of the ground a whole host of memories from my childhood and adolescent years came flooding back. Memories of my first visit to the East End with my schoolmates in 1975. A small affair of a Bristol Derby against the Rovers that resulted in a 1–1 draw with a goal for City from Paul Cheesley. My schoolmates were old hands regarding being in the East End but I will never forget the fear, excitement, and thrill of chasing after Rovers fans and not being entirely sure of what to do if I caught one. There is no doubt That afternoon will always stay with me, it was almost a right of passage to be out with your mates and not be governed by your parents. The East End is always talked about with affection, particularly by men of a certain age who will always come up with a story about the East End over a pint. So when I approached Bristol City with the idea to mark the passing of this iconic part of Ashton Gate. I was thrilled that they, like myself wanted to mark its passing in some way. The club acknowledge that this structure, although not much to look at, meant a lot to supporters over the years and although they will be replacing it with a fantastic new stand with state of the art facilities for supporters, they realise the spirit of the East End will always remain. I sincerely hope you enjoy reading these memories from supporters and players and I hope their tales will also show an insight into the different eras in which they are set. As Bristol City move to restructure Ashton Gate lets hope memories from this ground will never ever stop.

Neil Palmer

1.

THE EARLY YEARS

Queen Victoria lived just 26 days into the twentieth century. She died on the 26 January 1901 and the Britain she would leave behind would face some of the toughest years it could ever imagine. Albert Edward Prince of Wales was declared King Edward VII in 1902 and the decades that would follow would test every subject across this great land. Conflict in Europe would see Britain crash into the First World War in 1914, it would be a war that would decimate Europe in terms of infrastructure and more importantly lives. In total nine million combat troops and seven million civilians lost their lives across the war. Britain alone lost over one and a half million people. The end of the war in 1918 would see countries try and rebuild themselves both economically and politically. By 1920 economic output in the country fell by 25%, this was due to the financial instability of debt accumulated by the war. In the south-west of England unemployment stood at 15% and as the 1930s approached the great depression cut a swathe across the world as countries saw an economic down turn with more than three million unemployed across the UK.

The nineteen hundreds would see Bristol with 330,000 residents in the city. It was certainly on the up as a new Dock named The Royal Edward dock had been opened to advance the city's import and export trade. The main employers were Fry's chocolate and W.D. & H.O. Wills, who both had large factories across the city employing thousands. Both companies were also responsible for the growth in smaller companies who relied on them opening across the city. It was truly a city that was growing and in 1919 the council, in response to the housing act started work on building 'Village suburbs' such as Knowle, Bedminster and Fishponds and by 1930 some 3,000 slum properties were cleared and their occupants rehomed as part of a major building project across the city. As a sport Football would also be growing in terms of popularity as the organizing body found their feet. The Football Association joined FIFA in 1906 and this set the game up for a more global support. But with the outbreak of the First World War football became suspended as players joined up too fight. This alone was not without incident as the sports of cricket and Rugby had stopped in 1914 as their players joined up, but football continued until 1915, a decision that caused uproar with some parts of society claiming that footballers were 'cowards'. The Football Associations defence was that the game was good for morale and in hindsight this was a view that seemed correct, as the game seemed more popular than ever as crowds grew and grew. The Football Association withdrew from FIFA in 1920 as their relationship became fraught with their European cousins. It appeared that their was an unwillingness to play against teams that the country had been at war with and they wanted protection from 'foreign influences' in what was essentially a British game. This decision, agreed by all the Home Nation Associations would see the UK sides play no part in the new World Cup competition that was started in 1930 in fact it would be 1950 before any of the Home Nations would take part in the event. At home the top teams were Newcastle United, Aston Villa and Blackburn Rovers with their top players earning £8 per week during the season and £6 a week during the summer months. Money was not bad compared to the average wage of £3.75 being earnt by the man in the street. But it was ridiculous that at some Wembley fixtures the FA paid the band more to play at half-time than it did to the players appearing. This injustice would take years to rectify. For Bristol City the 1900s would see the birth of the club.

Just before the turn of the century Bristol South End amalgamated with Bedminster and essentially the club was born. The club alternated games between Bristol South Ends ground at St Johns Lane and Bedminster's at Ashton Gate. This continued until 1904 when the club opted for a move to Ashton Gate. The ground was blessed with the number one grandstand on the site of the Williams stand today and the number two stand on the site of the Dolman. To the south of the ground was an end that had a capacity for 8,000 fans. This structure would be known as The covered end. In 1916 the end was damaged by gales and found to be unsafe, so a year later the club demolished it and it was not be replaced until 1928. The club paid for the new end by selling Albert Keating and Clarrie Bourton to Blackburn Rovers for £3,650. It was a move that would not be popular amongst fans but in light of this book it was one of the clubs shrewdest decisions as this is the structure we know today. On the pitch the Babes, as they were known, started life in Southern League Division One playing teams like Swindon Town, Tottenham Hotspurs and Southampton and although a relegation would befall them in 1901 they would find themselves back in Division One and playing an FA Cup Final against Manchester United at Crystal Palace by the end of the decade. Although the final would see City lose 1–0 in front of 72,000 fans it showed that they had the potential to be one of the countries top teams of the day. This period in time would also see the clubs first 'Superstar' Billy 'Fatty' Wedlock who became the second Bristol City player to play for England after Billy Jones in 1901. Wedlock became popular with the fans for his skill and determination and he is still remembered to this day. With the outbreak of the war City would find themselves in the Combination League and playing friendlies until the conflict in Europe ended. When it did four years later the club, like many football clubs, found themselves mourning the loss of some of their players. City lost Arthur Moss, Tommy Ware, Edwin Bourton, and A. Edwards all killed in action overseas. During the twenties the club would move between Division Three (south) and Division Two and this inconsistency would blight the club as they moved through the 1930s and the oncoming Second World war. Throughout this dark time City would struggle financially right up until the end of the Second World War. One high point in the decade would see the 'Robins' as they were now called smash their attendance record for a game at Ashton Gate. The match was against Portsmouth in the fifth round of the FA Cup. The Gate is reported as 42,885, but as the Gates were rushed by people who did not pay, the figure is more likely to have been 50,000 inside Ashton Gate that day.

My dad used to go to the City with his mates whenever he could. He got tickets for the Portsmouth FA Cup replay at Ashton Gate in 1935. But him and his ten mates could not get in the ground due to the massive crowd which was officially 42,000 but people reckon there was 50,000 plus in the ground that day. Not being put off they found a ladder and climbed on top of the covered end where they saw City win 2–0. When the game ended they found that the ladder had been removed. So they sat up there for a couple of hours until they were rescued (probably by the person who moved the ladder in the first place).

Terry Day
Season Ticket holder for over 50 years

I first went to see Bristol City with my granddad Bert in the 1960s. Bert loved the club and he passed his passion down from my dad and myself and my own kids. I found out that City were doing a book about the East End so I thought I would mention a tale my Granddad always told us. He was about 10 years old and he could not get a ticket for the famous cup replay against Portsmouth at Ashton Gate. His dad loved the City but he had to work on the Saturday at the docks so he could not take young Bert. Being the resourceful type my granddad went to the game anyway and smuggled himself in amongst the thousands of supporters who were trying to get through the gates at the back of the covered end. Unfortunately for my granddad he was elbowed in the face and had a bloody nose. He still could not get into the ground and sat outside feeling very sorry for himself as the game kicked off. Then a policeman on horseback who had been trying to control the crowd came up to him and asked if he was ok. They chatted for a bit then the policeman lifted him up and sat him on the horse in front of him. They then preceded to ride into the ground using the surrounding cinder track. When they reached the front of the covered end the policeman lifted him down and told him to sit on the track and watch the game, which he did with all the other thousands that day. The match was City's biggest ever crowd and my granddad always says he arrived at the game like a king. It's great that I can share his tale with other City fans.

Charlie Hawkins
One of a line of City fans

My dad always told stories of when he stood on the covered end watching the City. Dad used to go in the late 1920s and his favourite player was Bert Neesam. Even up to Dad's death in 1977 he always looked at City players and said *'There not a patch on Bert'*.

Billy Taylor

Although I am not a big Bristol City fan I felt I had to let you know about my dad Freddie Windsor. I thought it would be appropriate for a book about the East End. My dad was an apprentice Welder at a company called Allison & Way who were based in Avonmouth. They helped supply the steel work for the covered end when it was rebuilt in 1928. Dad used to tell me that a lorry would take steels from Avonmouth up to Ashton Gate on a daily basis and one round trip alone would take the driver four hours. Whenever we passed the City ground dad would say, *'There it is, I helped build that'*. He would then proceed to talk about all the rivets and how it went together like a meccano kit. Too be honest it got on me and my brothers nerves listening to it every time we passed the ground, but God how I would love to hear it now. Dad passed away in 1997 aged 87 years old. With all the publicity about the new ground I will make sure I am there when they take down the East End so I can take some photos as a keepsake to what my dad helped build. He would have loved to known he would be in a book.

Peter Windsor

FRED STANIFORTH

Fred Staniforth was born near Rotherham in 1884. The young outside-right was spotted playing for local club Kilnhurst before signing for League side Rotherham, A move to Mexborough Town followed before his transfer to Bristol City in 1906. Staniforth was a instant hit with the City fans, creating many goals for his fellow team mates. He was part of a formidable strike force of Billy Maxwell, Sam Gilligan, Andy Burton and Frank Hilton. A member of the team that played in the 1–0 FA Cup defeat at the hands of Manchester United in 1909. Fred also appeared in the top flight for City. He fell out of favour with City after they signed Willie Clark from Sunderland in 1910 and he struggled to regain his place. A subsequent move to Grimsby Town followed in 1911 where he made 67 appearances and scored 8 goals. He finished his career at Liverpool but struggled to find a place in the side appearing only three times for the club. Fred never forgot Bristol and he returned to the south-west where he retired. He died in 1955 aged 70.

FRED STANIFORTH
BRISTOL CITY: 1906–11
APPEARANCES: 134
GOALS: 14

I have always stood on the East End. I first went with my dad in the 1960s. Dad would always tell me about my granddad who also supported City and stood on the same terrace. Dad used to say that grammps was at the famous Portsmouth game when they had over 50,000 in the ground. Apparently my gramps, who would have been in his late teens at the time, had to climb up into the roof of the covered end/East End as people were pouring into the terrace. Dad said gramps didn't really even see the game there were so many people in the stand. I am really proud that I have been able to pass the love of the City down to my own kids and grandchildren. It's wonderful that my family have had a Chapple stood in the covered end for almost all of its life and I can't wait to keep that tradition going with the new stand.

Barry Chapple
Third generation City fan

BILLY 'FATTY' WEDLOCK

Billy Wedlock was Bristol City's first superstar. Born in Bristol in 1880 he mesmerized the Ashton Gate faithful with his tough no nonsense approach at the heart of the City defence. Standing at 5ft 5in what Wedlock lacked in height he more than made up for in courage and skill. He was an outstanding athlete who earnt the nickname 'Indian rubber man' due to his ability to turn and deceive. Billy played for England 26 times between 1907 and 1914 scoring two goals in that period. He also represented The Football League on many occasions against rival Leagues. A one club man Billy retired in 1921 and the club held a benefit match for him at Ashton Gate between a Bristol eleven against an international eleven which raised £8,000. After retirement Billy became landlord of the Wedlock's pub across the road from the ground, a position he held for 43 years before his death in 1965. Billy Wedlock may always be remembered as 'Fatty' Wedlock due to his stout appearance but to real City fans he is remembered as fondly as ever. He was the man who captained them to the FA Cup Final in 1909 and became an England regular whilst wearing the red shirt of City. The club decided to mark this great Robin in 1996 when the East End was christened The Wedlock Stand.

BILLY 'FATTY' WEDLOCK
BRISTOL CITY: 1900–21
APPEARANCES: 403
GOALS: 17

HERBERT BERT NEESAM

Bert Neesam was a popular wing half with City supporters either ends of the First World War. Born in Yorkshire in1892 Neesam was spotted by local amateur side Grangetown Athletic playing for his local youth team Brompton. After a successful spell with Athletic Bert joined Bristol City in 1913. A popular playmaker he was renown for always giving 100%, which is something the City fans have always asked for. Neesam was part of the 1922–23 promotion winning team that many feel was one of the best City teams ever. Bert continued at Ashton Gate after the war but left in 1928 to join Bath City. After he retired this proud Yorkshire man stayed in the area and played cricket for Long Ashton. Bert died in 1969 aged 77.

HERBERT BERT NEESAM
BRISTOL CITY: 1913–28
APPEARANCES: 281
GOALS: 18

My granddad always told a story of how he played against City for Bristol Dockers in 1916. His name was Jimmy Steele and they were beaten 2–0 by City. Jim was in a reserved occupation at the time, as he was needed at the city's docks and games like this were mainly organised for everybody's morale. Jim was a big City fan who stood on the East End right up to his death in the 1970s. I wanted to make sure his name was in the book as he loved City and that part of the ground. He always told people that he played against the City.

Edward Steele
Taunton

I have been a City fan all my life. I come from Bedminster so there was no way I was ever going to support the blue side of the city. My dad and his dad were always City fans and it was with my granddad that I went to my first City game way back in 1969 a 4–0 win over Blackburn Rovers. My dad worked most Saturdays so I would go with my granddad Cyril. We would stand on the East End and although it was a bit lively in those days Cyril was a creature of habit and to quote him: *'No bloody yobbos going to move me from the place'*. While we would watch the games he would always tell me about the time he watched City in the FA Cup against Portsmouth from the roof of the stand. He told me he was in his late teens and as he and his brother could not get a ticket for the game they, like many others climbed up onto the roof of the stand and watched the game. I always took the story with a pinch of salt until I saw a photo of that game and there were loads of people on the East End roof. I am quite proud to think one of them was him. That's why when I heard about the book I had to see if it could be included as he would of loved it. He died in 1991 and I still miss him.

Michael Griffin
Exiled red in Bournemouth

2.

THE FORTIES AND FIFTIES

As with most cities in the middle of the Second World War, Bristol and its citizens suffered at the hands of Germanys Luftwaffe. Bristol was a prime target with its docks and massive manufacturing industry. It is incredible to try and understand how terrified people would have been as they sat in their air raid shelters huddled together and not knowing if their houses and possessions would be there when the raid ended. A night raid on Bristol in November 1940 saw 5,000 incendary and 10,000 high explosive bombs dropped on the City. Within an hour there were over 70 fires burning across the area. There was substantial damage to areas such as Castle Park, Knowle, Brislington, Bedminster and Filton with around 1,300 people losing their life that night. To say these were tough times for the people of Bristol is an understatement to say the least. Football though was still popular as it gave fans an escape from the nightmare of the war and everything that went with it The average wage at the time was £270 per year and the cost of a game at Bristol City was 1s 6d which equates to 7.5p. As far as Bristol City were concerned football was suspended at the outbreak of the war as many players were called up for active duty. The club still played matches but in a popular regional league, with City playing the likes of Bristol Rovers, Plymouth, Cardiff City, Newport County and Swindon Town. The leagues lasted until the end of the war in 1945 when the full Football League started back up with City competing in the Football League Third Division South. The club certainly did not come through the war years unscathed with the main grandstand destroyed in an air raid in 1941. Although many fans at the time were disappointed that Hitler's Luftwaffe had not destroyed the opposite grandstand known as the cowshed as it was in a poor state even before the war. In that same year two bombs fell on the Ashton Gate pitch, which left such craters that games, had to be called off and those parts of the pitch would become prone to flooding years later. This incident saw many lives loss in the surrounding area of Bedminster including former City left-back Sandy Torrance who lived locally and perished along with his wife. But with money and steel so scares repairing the damage was not a priority for the club. So the grandstand could not be rebuilt until 1953. But there was a bright light at the end of Bristol City's tunnel in the shape of Business man Harry Dolman who joined the Ashton Gate board in 1939. Dolman an engineer by trade proved himself to be a shrewd businessman who would guide City onto bigger and better things to come in the years ahead. On the pitch there were rumblings when City's talented Roy Bentley was sold to Newcastle United for £8,000 in 1945, as many fans thought Bentley was the heart of the team. Even without Bentley City made a good account of themselves through the forties with the prolific Don Clark upfront, This would cumulate in the 1946–47 season when Clark would set a record that will probably never be beaten, scoring 36 goals from 37 games. For supporters attendances boomed during the later stages of wartime football, which gave an indication into the huge interest that would prove so valuable to clubs during the austerity of the post-war era.

The 1940s would still remain a lasting legacy of the Second World War. Bristol City were averaging gates of around 16,000. This could be down to many factors such as you had a five-and-a half-day working week. You'd had the war and people did not have a lot of money in their pockets and going to football was their way of expressing themselves. By the early 1950s the national trend towards smaller attendances at football games became evident. There was a rise in real incomes, in fact the average wage had risen to £496 per year and a ticket in the covered end at Bristol City had also gone up to 1s 9d, which equates to 9p in todays money. Locally The Wills Company who made cigarettes and cigars were the main employers for most of south Bristol. By 1955 Wills were selling 100 million cigarettes a year. Figures like that would see a boom economically in the south Bristol area as people started to come out of the shadow of the war. There was an increase in the number of consumer options available for people to spend their money on.

The car and television were, without question, the most obvious agents of change in the leisure industry that football had now found itself in. Ashton Gate still showed the scars of Mr Hitler as it was reeling from post war scruffiness and austerity. But with Harry Dolman now in charge after being voted in as chairman in 1949,he made plans to bring the club forward. In 1953 Dolman pioneered the installation of floodlights, this is something we take for granted in todays football but back then it was revolutionary. Dolman designed them and being the shrewd businessman he was, his company Bracknell Dolman and Rogers built them at a cost of £3,500. These would later be unveiled and used for the first time in a game against Wolverhampton Wanderers in 1953 a game City would lose 4–1.

Dolman showed his skill as a negotiator when he sold the lights at a profit to Burton Albion years later. On the pitch Bristol Rovers were the top dogs in the city with their centre-forward Geoff Bradford seeing off all before him. Whilst the red half would see the first part of the 1950s in Division Three South and the later in the Second Division. It would not be long before the tables would be turned as a new lad from Wiltshire called John Atyeo, who had just signed for the club on £12 a week would become a terrace hero and make memories for players and fans alike.

JOHN ATYEO

John Atyeo will always be considered a 'One off' by the football fraternity. Not only for the way in which he lead the line for Bristol City with courage, skill and power but the way he lived his life away from the game choosing to stay part-time and working as a school teacher. Atyeo was adored by the City fans from the moment he made his debut for the club in 1951 against Newport County at Ashton Gate. And that affection remained right up to his death in 1993. Atyeo scored 341 goals for the club including a memorable one against Oldham Athletic in front of the covered end that clinched City's promotion to Division Two. After six caps for England and five goals to the good, it seems incredible that he was never picked again, many believe that this was due to the Football Association not being happy with his part-time status. Big clubs came calling but Big John was never interested in moving his family, when in terms of football even if he did sign for Manchester United the way the game was structured at that time meant he would get £20 a week no matter who he played for. Part of one of City's most exciting forward line of Atyeo, Clark,

Williams, Derrick, and Hooper. John certainly had no airs and graces about him he would lead by example and would never worry about who got the goals as long as it was City. Speaking before his own untimely death in 2010 Brian Clark said of Atyeo, *'He taught me everything I ever learned in the game, he talked me through games and took so much punishment during matches that it allowed me more freedom to get in the box. Off the field he was a gentleman and I miss him terribly.'* John passed away in 1993 and the club has since named a new stand that was built on the site of the old open end in his honour. Even though he retired from the game in 1966 City shirts can still be seen around the ground with Atyeo on the back, surely there can be no more fitting tribute than to be loved by the fans years after you played.

JOHN ATYEO
BRISTOL CITY: 1951–66
APPEARANCES: 647
GOALS: 351

The date was 8 Jan 1949 and City played Chelsea in a cup match. It was Roy Bentley's return to the Gate as he had had been transferred from City to Newcastle and now was captain of Chelsea, needless to say he scored two of the goals in a 3–1 Chelsea win. I was 16 and not very tall, there was a crowd of 36,454 and I was wearing a gabardine mac and so climbed a stanchion at the back of the East End and tied myself with my belt to it so I was able to watch the match even if it was a bit uncomfortable.

Roy Day

I remember being on Christmas leave from the army in 1940. I decided to go down the Gate with my brother-in-law Bill. We were big City fans and didn't get to see them as much due to the war. We had a few drinks before the game and then went into the East End. I remember it was a great game as City beat Southampton 6–2. Bill and I continued to drink as Bill had a bottle of whisky in his over coat. When the game ended we were very much worse for wear and decided to sit on one of the walls to the back of the ground until we sobered so as not to go home too drunk. We must have fallen asleep as I was woken when I fell off the wall and into somebody's garden cutting my head and hurting my foot. Bill eventually got me home in a wheelbarrow we stole from a garden. My God we got into trouble when we got home.

Bert Richards

I loved it in the East End. I loved the singing and the atmosphere. We used to go drinking at the Bell in Bedminster before the game. It was a chance to forget all our worries and get together and shout for the City. My favourite was Don Clark he was fantastic in front of goal. And when his son Brian joined the club I used to sit in the Williams stand and cheer him on although he wasn't as good as Don.

Arthur Strong
Bedminster

I never really went to football when I was a kid but when I came out of the army in 1948 a group of us decided to start going down the Gate to see City. We would meet up in North Street and have a couple of beers and do a sweepstake on who would score the first goal. If you won you won a pound and you could do a lot with a pound then. We would all be singing and shouting in the East End and if a bloke came in with a little kid we would pass him down towards the front and over the barrier where the police would put him behind the goal so he would not get crushed...I loved it.

Albert Summers
90-year-old Bristol City fan.

I remember watching City beat Sheffield United 5–1. It was a bitterly cold day. The date was about 1956 I think. I got chatting to a bloke in the East End who like me was a regular. He had a Jack Russell puppy under his coat and I bought it off him at half-time. I can't remember how much I paid or why he had it. My missus went mad when I brought the dog home but the kids loved her. We called her Poppy. We had her 14 years. People never believed me that I bought a dog in the East End.

Cyril Williams
City Fan

The 1950s were a wonderful time to go to football at the city. I was only a kid but I remember it all. Watching John Atyeo, Ivor Guy, and Ernie Peacock, I was in awe of them. I used to go with my dad in the East End and he would put me up at the front so I could see the game. It was one of the few things I could do with dad as he was always working, so it was very special for me. I still went to the East End up until the early eighties. My dad died in 1968 and every time I stood on that terrace I thought of him. I know it has changed over the years but I will shed a tear for dad when it gets knocked down.

Brian Forrell
Lifelong City fan

I remember being in the East End and watching a game against the Rovers in the 1950s. City were on the attack and as the ball came towards the goal and Rovers player Jackie Pitt knocked it out of play with his arm. We all saw it and in unison all screamed 'HANDBALL'. As the ref ran towards Jackie he gestured that he knocked it out with his chest, the ref gave City a corner. With that Jackie turned to us all in the East End and stuck two fingers up at us. We all went mental. It makes me laugh when I think about it today.

Malcolm Pearce
City Fan

I always loved Tony Cook; it was probably because I stood right behind his goal in the East End. I used to get to the ground a couple of hours early so I could get to my usual place behind the goal. Tony always waved to us when he ran to the goal at the start of the match and I loved it. My lasting memory is a game against West Ham in 1956. It was near the end of the season and we drew 1–1. At the end of the game Tony grabbed a small brown paper bag that he had in his goal. He came behind his goal and grabbed some mints from the bag and threw them into the crowd. I managed to catch some and I was so thrilled that I promised myself that I would keep them forever but I ate them on the way back home to Knowle.

Peter Skipton
City fan who still eats too many sweets

ALEC EISENTRAGER

Alec Eisentrager was truly taken to the Bristol City fans hearts. It seems incredible that a couple of years after the Second World War, Alec decided to make his life here in Britain, Admittedly he came to this country not of his own accord but there was something about this country and its fans that found a place in his heart. This diminutive striker scored over 200 goals for Trowbridge Town and it was this vein of form that sparked the interest of Bristol City after a trial at the club. This skilful forward certainly hit the ground running with four goals in a 6–0 victory over Newport County within weeks after signing for the Robins in the 1949–50 season. Alec was a real showman and he gave a different dimension to the City attack and it was testimony to Alec, his City team mates, and above all the fans at Ashton Gate that after his career ended with City he stayed amongst the people of Bristol who loved him and made him feel welcome. After City Alec played for Merthyr Tydfil whilst still living in Bristol. He then turned out for local Bristol team Westbury Park on the Durdham Downs until he hung up his boots in the early 1960s.

I was born in Hamburg Germany. Which is not a million miles away from Bristol but it might as well have been when I st on the path of football. I was on the books of SV Hamburg and played with the likes of Uwe Seeler who captained West Germany in the 1966 World Cup. At the age of 17 I joined the Luftwaffe and fought for my country. I was taken prisoner by the British in the Netherlands and brought to the UK as a POW. When the war ended I stayed in England and played for Trowbridge Town and it was there that I got spotted for Bristol City. I signed for City in 1950 and fell in love with the club and its supporters. I will always remember scoring four goals for City against Newport County in a 6–0 win, Those were my first goals for the club and the reaction I got from the fans will always be special too me. The East End made a noise like no other and the fans of City will always be special, I still find it wonderful that there were obviously men I had fought against in the war cheering me on in a Bristol City shirt and that is something that will always be dear in my heart. I am sad that the East End will be going as it was always the end I liked to attack and score in front of especially the reaction of those lovely City fans.

ALEC EISENTRAGER
BRISTOL CITY: 1949–58
APPEARANCES: 240
GOALS: 47

I have always loved the East End. It's the excitement and involvement of standing with your own fans at one end of the ground with the team coming towards you. I first went with my dad in the 1950s and I loved being squashed in with everybody and the smell of drink and cigarettes was what it was all about. I got so excited if I got just a glimpse of the match. One game in particular sticks in my mind and it was 1956 and we beat Rovers 5–3 with Johnny Atyeo scoring two. It was always good to beat the gas and I think I got up early for school on the Monday so I could give some stick to the few Rovers fans we had in the playground. I will be sad to see the East End go.

John Boulder
City fan for over 50 years.

I met my wife in the East End. It was the late 1950s and I used to go with my mates and we would stand to the right of the pitch which is now the family stand. Every game I would see these two sisters with their dad watching the game. I was attracted to the older one as she was about my age. Over the course of the seasons I would get chatting to her and her dad Stan about the game. I found out that her name was Maureen and she lived in the Knowle area of Bristol which was not too far from my home at

Totterdown. I plucked up the courage to ask her out and we went to the Glen where they had dancing. After a few weeks I asked her to marry me and we have been married for 55 years. So thanks East End!!!

Tommy and Maureen Reynolds
Still in love after all these years

My Brother Tony and me always went to the East End when we watched Bristol City. We used to cycle from our house in Barton Hill and leave the bikes with a bloke my dad worked with called Bill in Gerald Road. He would look after them for us while we watched the game. Great Memories!!

Ivor Williams
Thanks Bill

I have been going to the City for years and it seems so different to when I used to go in the fifties. I would stand in the East End with my mates and you would be pushed and shoved all over the place but nobody ever got angry or had a fight, we just got on with things. If it ever did get heated it was only due to the fact that a little kid might be getting crushed or squashed, if that happened we were just passed down to the front out of danger.

Alan Ricketts
East Ender

I feel compelled to tell you of a story my late dad always told us as kids. He was a regular at the City in the 1940s. He went on a bit of a pub crawl with some mates in and around Bedminster. On arrival at our house in Dampier Road in the early hours of the morning he attempted to wake my mum as he could not find his key. My mum opened the bedroom window and told him too 'Bugger off' and come back when he was sober. He pleaded for forgiveness but my mum was having none of it. My dad then realised that he needed somewhere to sleep so he headed for the Winterstoke Road bus depot to see if he could blag his way into sleeping in one of the buses parked up for the evening. But his drunken ramblings to the watchman on site got him nowhere. He then hit on a plan and that was to steal a blanket off a neighbours washing line and climb into Bristol City's East End and go to sleep, and this is exactly what he did. Dad set off and broke into the end and settled down at the back of the terrace. He woke in the morning and came back home to more grief from my mum after he told her he had slept with someone he loved. My dad told that story right up to his death in 1995. He actually did sleep overnight in the East End.

Alan Humphries
Bedminster

I loved going to the City with my dad in the 1950s. My favourite player was Ernie Peacock. I used to love it when he came crunching in for a tackle. I used to stand in the East End with dad and all the men around us would shout

'Go on Ernie'. He was ferocious on the pitch but I remember getting his autograph outside the ground, he smiled and ruffled my hair. I will never forget it. I could not wait to show my mates in school on the Monday morning. I still have the autograph book all these years later.

Mike Sully
City fan of over 50 years

My memories of the East End will be working with my dad. He was a painter with Pentalls who were a painting and decorating company in south Bristol. We were big City fans in our house so dad was thrilled when he was part of a gang sent to paint some parts of Ashton Gate. I remember it being boiling hot in the late 1950s. He took me with him on a couple of days, mainly to keep me out of trouble but I loved helping out although I came home with more paint on me than on Ashton Gate. Dad and his workmates would sit on the terraces at the East End and have their lunch and I would sit with them looking out at the ground. When I look back now it was a magical time, and I know the East End has changed over the years but I will think about those times when they knock it down. I will be sorry to see it go.

Archie Thompson
City fan and retired Painter and decorator (like my dad)

My Dad Terry was a St John Ambulance man and he attended both City and Rovers games on alternating Saturdays. When he worked at the City he would often sit in front of the East End. He told us one story of Mike Thresher the uncompromising defender. Aparently dad had to come on to the pitch to carry off a Cardiff City player who Thresher had given one of his 'special' tackles to. As the game had stopped Thresher was stood over the player and he recognised my dad from the match the week before against Bristol Rovers at Eastville. Thresher said to my dad, '*I remember you from last week didn't you help carry my mate Harold (Jarman) off when I tackled him?*' My dad laughed his head off.

Peter Buckingham
Clevedon

I will always remember the first game under floodlights against Wolves in 1953. I remembers Wolves beat us 4–2 I think but it was so exciting to see a match under the lights. The player's just looks so different and the way the red and the gold of the shirts stood out in the lights made it very special. I was only young but I can still remember some men stood around by me saying '*This will never catch on*'. Which is hilarious when you think of it today. I remember there was something magical about all of us coming out of the East End en masse into the dark. I had to walk all the way home to Knowle and when I got home my mum just said '*Billy is that you?*' And that was that. Now they would have a search party out bearing in mind I was only about eight. Even today I prefer night games at the Gate especially with my son and grandson. But I will never forget that game against Wolves.

Billy Finchlay
City Fan

All my family throughout the years have been Bristol City fans, in fact my great-granddad was one of the 75,000 that saw City lose 1–0 to Manchester United in the 1909 Cup Final at Crystal Palace so I was always going to be a red. As a family we always went into the East End but back then it was called the covered end. My first memories are of going to games was in the fifties by coach. I lived in Fishponds and many supporters from north Bristol would in those days hire a coach as not many people had cars. The coach would stop off in Fishponds and Kingswood and take supporters to Ashton Gate. When we arrived some of the men would go straight in the Star pub opposite the ground which was owned by former City Legend Billy 'Fatty' Wedlock for a few pints. I would get to the front of the East End but I was always too small to see properly so one time my dad decided to take a tin for me to stand on which I did until I grew tall enough to see unaided. Over the years I have seen many great City players and games from the East End but my favourite was always John Atyeo, I wonder what sort of money he would be worth today? I have always gone in the East End and it is a special place for me. I sit with people that are my mates for 90 minutes and its funny that I know nothing of their own lives or their families but see them every other Saturday down the Gate. I will be sad when it goes but I suppose we all have to move on.

Terry Hamblin
City fan for over 50 years

The match I will always remember whilst watching in the East End or covered end as it was then, was the FA Cup 4th round tie between City and Blackpool in the 1958–59 season. I was 10 years old at the time and was one of the 42,000 that packed into Ashton Gate. We lived in Bridgewater Somerset and my dad used to take me and my brother to City or Rovers depending on what great players were turning out for the opposition at the time. So when City drew Blackpool in the cup the thought of watching Stanley Matthews was a no brainer as far as my dad was concerned. Me, Dad and my brother boarded the train bound for Bristol Temple Meads excited about what lay ahead. Dad told us stories of how great Matthews was and I could not wait for the game to start. We then got the bus to the ground and the crowd was unbelievable. Dad put me and my brother on the crash barriers while he stood at the back of the covered end. All of a sudden there was a massive surge and the whole crowd moved as one like a huge river. My brother and me were squashed against the fencing behind the goal. Fortunately for us the St John Ambulance people behind the goal managed to get all the kids out and onto the touch line where they placed wooden benches for us to sit on. It was a frightening experience looking back but it was worthwhile when Stanley Matthews came and took a corner and I was sat about four feet from him. It's a memory I will never forget.

Derek Pitcher
Bridgewater

I first went to the City in the 1940s during the war. I was only a nipper but I loved going. Me and my brother Walter always stood in the covered end. It was first place we ever stood so that's where we stayed until the 60s when we got a season ticket for the Williams stand. I seem to remember it was a shilling to get in but we could not afford a programme, but if we found one on the floor it was like finding gold dust. I loved standing behind the goal that feeling of the team coming towards you always gave me a thrill.

Bert Loveday
City fan

It was a different era when I first went to City. My dad took me to my first game which was a reserve game against Cardiff back in the 1950s. I can remember sitting on a crash bar in the covered end with my dad and there being a couple of thousand in the ground. You have to remember that in those days nobody went to away games so loads of people turned out to see the reserves. When I look back and think how the game has changed it makes me smile, bookings were a real talking point and I remember my dad and his mates talking for ages about someone being booked, it was a really big thing back then. Also there would be groups of men just like today but if there was some swearing somebody would say; 'Hang on lads there's kids about here' and the swearing would stop. It was the same if some of the lads got a bit rowdy with each other you could bet somebody would sort it out themselves.

Billy Hobbs
City fan

I loved standing in the covered end when I was a kid in the 50s. If it moved you went with it. If it moved forward so did you. I don't know about some people but my mates and me used to think sometimes cor this is a bit dodgy. It was so tight in there you couldn't even get something out of your pocket. I used to try and have a fag but it was too tight to get it out of my jacket and light it. For those that did smoke they would find themselves locked in a large cloud of smoke all game. Also there was not many police about at the grounds, and those that were there you would see them every other week and say hello to them, if they got in the way at a game while you were watching someone would always shout; 'Sit down' or 'take your hat off'. There are many games I remember watching City at the time from the covered end, but one that always stays in my memory was in the 1955 season against Rovers. We arrived late and there must have been 40,000 in Ashton Gate and they would not let me and my mate into the covered end as it was too crammed. We panicked as we thought we couldn't get in and the noise from the crowd was amazing. Thank God a copper took pity on us and got us into the front of the Williams stand, but we still missed the kick-off. I remember thinking how weird the covered end looked from another part of the ground as we had always stood on it and had never seen it from that angle before. I loved the old covered end and will miss it but I will always have the memories.

Alan King
covered end fan

My memory of the Wedlock stand, covered end or East End call it what you will. Was in the 1954–55 season. I was 10 years old and I used to go to games with my dad. I remember the crowds seemed huge and we always used to go into the covered end. I loved the noise and the atmosphere as it was magical for a youngster. This particular game was against Watford on 13 November. The reason I remember the date will be evident in this story. My mum was expecting her second child and my brother or sister. Dad took me to the City game and the Robins won 1–0 with a goal from Jack Boxley my favourite player at the time. After the game I sat outside the pub in North Street while my dad and his friends shared a few drinks to celebrate. I got a lemonade and some nuts if I remember. We then walked back home too Hotwells. On arrival our next door neighbour Mrs Finchley came out in a right state telling me and dad that mum had gone into her house as she did not feel well and had gone into labour in the front room. Dad and me rushed in only to be presented with mum holding a baby brother for me. I was subsequently given an orange juice by Frank Finchley and then told the news that the baby was to be called Jack. Dad thought it was fitting as Jack Boxley had scored the goal that afternoon. So that's how my brother Jack came into this world and was named after my favourite City player. Thank God it had not been a girl, as God knows what dad had called her. I have spent many wonderful years stood in the East End with my little brother Jack and we always have a laugh about that game against Watford.

Thomas Winfred
City fan for life

I first started going to Bristol City in the mid fifties with my dad. I seem to remember it cost about one shilling for me and half a crown for my dad. We would always walk to the ground from our house in Bedminster and I used to love the crowd all moving towards Ashton Gate. I don't think people realise that you would get about 20,000 at games and almost nobody had a car, so we would all arrive en masse and leave en masse. Many a time I would hold my dad hands as hard as I could so I wouldn't get separated from him. I have many memories of watching City from the covered end as it was then. I think my lasting memory is the 1958 4–1 demolition of neighbours Rovers. I remember Geoff Bradford got the first goal for Rovers and all the men in and around me at the covered end getting more and more agitated. A glancing header from Bobby Etheridge put us level and we all went mental. John Atyeo got our second and goals from Curtis and Etheridge made it 4–1. I don't know what the attendance was but it felt like a 100,000 to a youngster like me. I will always remember City getting presented with the Gloucester Cup and running round the pitch. I don't really think it registered that this was a cup just for Bristol teams, as far as I was concerned City were the best team ever as they had just won a cup.

Douglas Ford
City fan

Happy memories of standing in the covered end with my dad, brothers, sons, friends and even grandkids. I have supported Bristol City since the early 1950s when I went with my dad as a six-year-old. My first game was 52–53 seasons and it was a 0–0 draw with Milwall, but I still went back with my dad. Early memories of those days was always walking from our house along the feeder with my dad and calling in for my Uncle Tom who lived in Raleigh road. I was always fascinated by a man who lived a couple of doors up from Uncle Tom. He had a kind of corrugated garage but like many people of the time no car. He would charge people one shilling to leave their bikes in his garage and he must have made a small fortune on match days as it seemed everybody arrived by bike. I have always stood on the covered end watching City even in the seventies when it was a bit scary with the football violence. But I always made sure myself and my sons were well away from the trouble. Through the eighties I continued to stay at that part of the ground, as I always loved the atmosphere it generated. As my sons grew up they would go and stand with their mates but into the last stages of the ground when the seating went in we would all sit together, my sons, my two grandsons and me. I am sad that this part of City's heritage has gone but I see the need for better facilities at Ashton Gate and even though I am now in my seventies I still find the new stand very exciting as I know it will be fantastic.

Arnold Wilson
Life long City fan

When I heard they were redeveloping the East End, as I have always known it I immediately thought about my mum and dad. We have always been massive City fans in our household. My mum and dad took my sister and me to games in the late 60s and I have carried on the tradition with my own children although my sister now lives in Canada with her family. Mum and dad were both from Brislington and even at a young age they had a love for football and Bristol City. They went to the same school and were childhood sweethearts who went to games with my dad's father. Dad told me the first game he saw with my mum was the start of the 1951–52 seasons and it was a 3–1 victory for City against Newport County and goals from Atyeo, Rodgers and Williams. Mum and dad continued to go to games and eventually went on their own and had their special place to stand by the turnstile in the then covered end. The reason this part of the ground was so special to my parents is because it was here in 1958 in front of a backdrop of City beating Brighton 3–0 that dad asked mum to marry him during the game. She said yes and the rest they say is history. They continued to go to games both together and with us kids. Sadly mum passed away in 1993 and dad found it too painful to go to Ashton Gate as he said it would not be right without his beloved Angela by his side. Dad passed away in 1999. I have always had a soft spot for the old East End as I looked across from my seat in the Williams stand with my children by my side and I always tell them that's where nan and gramps used to go. So the redevelopment will be tinged with sadness as they pull it down but I'm sure mum and dad would have approved.

Michael Ullman
For my mum and dad

JACK BOXLEY

The Ashton Gate fans may well remember Jack Boxley for his sublime left foot; many thought he could undo the laces on a football with it. But Boxley was much more than a skilful City winger. Signed by City manager Pat Beasley from non-league Stourbridge in 1950. The £2,000 cheque the midland club received was a decent price for a non-league player and many must have thought that Boxley was not worth the money. Beasley backed his and the boards judgement and Boxley became an instant hit. Jack was a real match winner and although he wasn't the most ferocious in the tackle he would become part of a legendary front line that included Arnold Rodgers and John

Atyeo providing goalscoring opportunities for City's front two men with some incredible service. His friendship on and off the field with Atyeo would end up with him being big John's best man at his wedding. Boxley became an integral part of City's promotion winning side of 1954–55 scoring 11 goals in the process. In 1956 Boxley along with Jimmy Rodgers moved to Coventry City returning two years late although he was past his prime and with the youngster Jantzen Derrick storming through the ranks. Jack would retire at the end of the 1960–61 season staying in Bristol where he lives to this day.

I always wanted to be a footballer and when I left the army I joined Stourbridge in the non-league. It was a dream come true for me to join a professional club like Bristol City. I know there were many teams interested in me but I was happy to go south. I did not know anything about Bristol as a City but I loved it as soon as I arrived. I loved playing in front of the City fans and in particularly the covered end. That part of the ground always seemed to generate the atmosphere that went around the ground. I have many memories about playing at Ashton Gate. And of course the fans. I remember as you came out of the tunnel it would always get boggy when it rained in that area and that was apparently due to a bomb that had landed there in the war. Another memory I have was a guy in the covered end who would always shout out at me when I beat a full-back 'Tell him he's rubbish Jack'. It always made me laugh and I am sorry I never met him. Obviously the promotion was a special moment for me as I felt we had a real top side then and we could give anybody a game at that time. But the one match that sticks in my mind was a game against Watford when our 'keeper Tony Cook had to go off injured and as there were no subs City's full-back Ivor Guy went in goal and had a stormer. They battered us and we battered them. The covered ends were incredible that day as they gave us and particularly Ivor such fantastic support. Then I got my chance from a pass from Jimmy Rodgers and blasted the ball into the net from 20 yards to win the game for City. I thought the place was going to erupt it's a memory I will never forget. I was sad to leave the club but when I look back I made the City of Bristol my home and I have loved every minute of it. I will be sad to see that part of the ground demolished but as with anything clubs have to move on if they want to compete and that's what we all want for Bristol City.

JACK BOXLEY
BRISTOL CITY: 1950–56, 1960–61
APPEARANCES: 213
GOALS: 35

I am in my seventies now but think the idea of this book is wonderful. I always used to stand on the covered end when I first went to go and see Bristol City as a 10-year-old way back in 1953. It was a family affair with my dad and his three brothers all walking to the game from our house in Brislington. The streets would get rammed with people before and after the game as not many people in those days had cars so you either walked or went by bus. I have always stood on the covered end, as this is where my dad first took me and I have always felt at home watching from that part of the ground, even in the scary days of the 1970s when it became the East End. I eventually moved with my sons and grandchildren to the Dolman stand in the late eighties, although I am still a stones throw from my old pitch to the left of the goal in the East End. I have seen many great games from the terraces as I am sure most City fans have and also I have had the privilege to see some wonderful players grace the red shirt over the years notably John Atyeo, Brian Clark, Chris Garland and Gerry Gow. In fact the list is endless. And it is funny when you recall what stays in your memory. Mine is when I walked to the game with my family and about two miles from the ground City player Tommy Burden jumped off the bus with his bag and walked along with us to the ground. He laughed and joked with my dad and his brothers and he even ruffled my hair as all the grown ups chatted. I was in shock and I couldn't believe I was walking along with a real life footballer. We wished Tommy all the best and told him we would be behind the goal. The game was against Leicester City around 1955 and City drew 1–1 with Tommy scoring City's goal. When he scored he waved to the covered end but my dad and his brothers and especially me thought the wave was for us. I couldn't wait to tell all my school friends how I met Tommy Burden. After that meeting I would always slow down a bit when walking with my dad in case the bus pulled up, which it did frequently but Tommy never got off the bus and I never did get to walk with him. I met him years later at a charity dinner at the Dolman stand and he laughed about how I remembered things. It was a memory that I will never forget. I feel sad that the ground will be losing that part of its history but hopefully it can make new memories for the new generation like my grandsons.

Billy Solomon
City fan

When I was a youngster I used to work for a painting company in Bristol called William Samuel Morris. They were based in East Street, Bedminster and they got the contract every summer to provide the paint along with materials to Bristol City so their apprentices could freshen the ground up before the season started. This was a great job if you were a City fan, as along with material our foreman Bill Thomas would take some lads to guide the apprentices in their duties. Being a City fan I always made sure I would volunteer for the work that lasted around four weeks. I used to love it chatting to them as they were more or less my age and we used work and have our lunch together. It was a fantastic time with the sun shining sat with some of the young City lads particularly in the covered end of the ground. On many occasions I would go out with them on a night to the Glen nightclub and even pretend to the young ladies that I played football for a living although looking back they were more impressed when I told them I was an apprentice painter as I was getting more money than them. How times have changed. I have some great memories of the covered end and when I stood in it I would always get ribbed by my mates if the paintwork was not up to scratch.

Danny Colum
City fan

I have to tell the story of my grandfather. He was a City supporter and I remember going to games with him during the 1970s and sharing many great times with him on the East End, in particular that famous night against Portsmouth when the club won promotion to the top flight. My gramps name was Bill and he always told me about the game against Aston Villa in 1943. He was a youngster at the time and he went with his dad and two brothers. Dad was home from the army and he took the boys to the game as a treat. Apparently there were around 30,000 in Ashton Gate for this wartime fixture that ended 0–0. You could not move in the covered end where they were positioned and just before the end of the game City had a chance through Roy Bentley and the whole of the crowd swayed forward and my granddad disappeared amongst the crowd. He just kept moving forward and was eventually picked up from the wall around the pitch by a policeman. His father was frantic looking for him along with his two brothers who had managed to stay with his dad. As the final whistle went and everybody filed out my great grandfather was shouting 'Billy' all around the outside of the ground. Granddad was eventually reunited with his family and his dad wacked him across the head for getting lost. Granddad always laughed because the policeman said, 'You deserved that,' as his dad hit him. My granddad was a wonderful man who loved City and he would be thrilled to think that this story he told every time he went in the covered end was in a book.

Chris Madden
In memory of Billy Madden

Many thanks for giving me the opportunity to add some memories to a book about a part of the ground that I have spent hours at over the years. I first started going to the covered end in the 1950s with my dad and I followed this through the sixties and the seventies although it was a bit rough in there during those times especially the seventies when the football violence emerged. I still went though as I had mates there that I made from the fifties. If I had to pick a game it would have to be the 1–1 FA Cup draw with Blackpool in 1959. As I always stood behind the goal my favourite City player was 'keeper Tony Cook. I used to watch his every move and when I went home I would dive around my front room saving a rolled up sock as my brother took penalties against me.

I remember the Blackpool game, as all the talk was about Stanley Matthews turning out for Blackpool and appearing at the Gate. The crowd was massive and I am lead to believe there were 43,000 at Ashton Gate that day. I still remember the crowd in the covered end as I squeezed into a spot with my mates. I couldn't really see much of the game due to the crowd but every now and then I could see Tony Cook diving about and the crowd cheering him. Then City scored with Bert Tindall and everybody went wild. I fell on the floor and some men picked me up and I re-joined my mates. I have to say I never got a glimpse of Stanley Mathews on the pitch that day but I did join the crowds of supporters who waited for a glimpse of the great man as he left to board the Blackpool coach. He waved as the supporters cheered him (things were so polite in those days). I will never forget the size of that crowd squeezed into the covered end.

Ivor Harold
City fan for years

I love the City and even though I am in my 70s I loved the covered end. When I was a kid in the fifties I would sit on a crash barrier and was held there by my brother. In those days scarves and rattles were the order of the day. There was no singing or chanting just polite cheering. No cursing and certainly no swearing. In later years you screamed from the moment you got in there until the moment you left. I never had a voice at the end of the game. It was amazing being in that old covered end under the roof, you would scream your head off and it would be just deafening, like thunder rolling around. I loved the noise and atmosphere at that end. These days I sit in the grandstand and sometimes have a meal before the game. I always look at that end of the ground and think about the best days of supporting City was in that end with my mates. I will be sad to see it go but I understand why the club are doing it.

You have to move with the times and you can't give people crap facilities forever.

Alan Dorning
Life long City fan

Many thanks for asking people for their own personal memories of the covered/East End. I suppose you can always tell the era of the person by how they refer to that part of the ground. The old boys like myself say covered end, then middle aged blokes say East End and the youngsters say the Wedlock. My own memories are of the covered end. I used to work for the City on match days and I would have the job of collecting the money from the turnstiles at the covered end and bringing it to underneath the main Grandstand to be counted, its incredible really how everything was done visually and all loose change was just put in a bag and carried around. I know there are stories about turnstile blokes having a few quid for themselves, but I don't believe that and certainly did not happen when I was working, although to be honest nobody would of known any different, but I did used to let blokes I knew in for free (sorry Mr Lansdown). I became quite skilful at looking around the ground and guessing how many was in the ground. And we would have bets amongst the other turnstile operators to guess the match attendance. I always remember the covered end being full no matter who City were playing. I suppose it was a real base for all the fans to meet up in and talk about their week and of course get away from the missus for a couple of hours.

Michael Allen

I hope you enjoy my personal memory of the covered end. I have been watching Bristol City for over 60 years and in that time I have had many good and loads of bad memories of going to see the men in red. This particular memory comes from 1957. I was 19 years of age and I was working at W.D. Wills in Bedminster. Every Saturday a group of employees, both male and female would meet in North Street for coffee then make our way to Ashton Gate to watch the City. There were eight of us in the party of which three were girls, one of which was a vision of loveliness called Annette. It was stood in the covered end during a match against Fulham in 1955 just after John Atyeo had scored that I had first kissed Annette and from then we were basically joined at the hip. We were going out together whilst still part of the group and we continued to go and watch the City. I knew she was the one for me and we talked about getting married and settling down together. The game in question was against Notts County in the October of 1957. I was deciding whether to ask Annette to marry me all the way through the game when City were awarded a penalty. This is my moment I thought. If Johnny Watkins scores this I will ask her and if he misses, well I don't know what I will do. Johnny buried the penalty as City won 3–0. Everyone was jumping up and down celebrating and as I was holding Annette I asked her to be my wife. She screamed yes and all our friends and some complete strangers started cheering and patting us on the back. We were married in 1958 and Annette had red and white flowers as hats off to City. We were married for over 50 years before Annette passed away in 2012. We celebrated our 50th Anniversary sat in the Wedlock stand watching City along with all our family and friends, it was a wonderful day. My son and Grand-sons are big City fans, which I suppose is only natural although I don't really go to many games these days. I will shed a tear when the bulldozers come in and demolish that part of the ground, but I will always have memories of my darling wife and the spot where she agreed to be my wife. Thanks again for allowing me to share my story for this book.

Walter Hughes

My first ever experience of Ashton Gate and the cov-ered end was in 1958 and a friendly against French side Bordeux. I still have no recollection of why the fixture was being played and I know that when I tell people of the fixture they are fascinated that City played a foreign team back in those days, but I seem to remember loads of friendlies against German and French teams. I was only about 14 years old back then and I went to the game with some friends who had just started to go to games at the City so when I was asked I jumped at the chance. We waked from Dartmoor street in Bedminster where we all lived and piled into the covered end. I can't remember exactly what the attendance was but to me it seemed like the place was packed. One of my lasting memories that made me and my friends laugh all the way home was a man at the front of the terracing who kept shouting 'Dirty Froggies' every time one of the Bordeaux players touch the ball. We kept shouting that for years after and even today when I see some of my old muckers who are in their seventies we still shout 'Dirty Froggies'. It was a great time for football with some wonderful players. Oh and for the record City won 2–0 with goals from John Atyeo, it was a great day

Hugh Winterstone
City fan

If I had to pick a game to remember the covered end it would have to be the first night game under the floodlights at Ashton Gate in 1953. I know people don't even think about it now but this a massive thing for the club and in particular a game against Wolverhampton Wanderers who were a top side. Their gold shirts against the night sky still are vivid in my mind to this day. City got beat 4–1 (I think) but the excitement of that night and walking home with my dad and getting fish and chips almost brings a tear to my eye. I have always preferred night games and I believe the covered end was better on night games, it just seemed a better atmosphere. All my mates played football on Saturday afternoons so they would only make night games and over the years we always had a great time. But nothing will ever beat that walk down North Street with my late father all those years ago and suddenly seeing the floodlights on and Ashton Gate all lit up like a church. It was magical and something I will never forget. I can understand why City want to move on and make Ashton Gate better for the fans with the building of the new stand. I have not been to the Gate for years as I live abroad, but thank you for the opportunity for sharing my memories of my favourite part of the ground.

Tony Cornell
Exiled City fan living in Spain

With the demolition of the covered end I was really pleased to here about City's idea to put peoples stories together for this book. I hope I get included in the final publication. I have stood on the covered end for at least 30 years on and off. I was very sad from a traditional point of view when they put the seats in during the late 90s but I suppose I could understand why after the football tragedies and if I'm honest I was getting to the point where I needed a sit down during a game. As I said I have seen many games from that part of the ground. And when it comes to remembering your favourite game, well I suppose it's like remembering the first record you bought everybody remembers his or her first game. Mine was 1950 and Christmas Day. City beat Plymouth Argyle 1–0 and if I remember Boyd scored the goal for City. The game was a Christmas treat and I walked to the match with my dad, uncles and cousins. I then started to go to City regularly and I think my happiest time was when I worked for W.D. Wills in Bedminster like so many from that area. I would finish work at 12pm on Saturday lunch time and go with my mates straight into the Rising Sun pub where we would have a few drinks then go and watch City and win, loose or draw go home, get dressed and go straight up the glen nightclub. We would be stood in the covered end planning our Saturday night out with the precision of a military movement. When I look back you would see loads of blokes like myself all in their work clothes as they had just finished for the morning and gone straight on to the City ground. I know I have seen better days watching City than the 1950s but they were a special time in my life and it all revolved around that wonderful club.

Alan Prentice
City fan forever

I have many memories of going to Ashton Gate and in particularly the covered end as I have always referred to it. I used to go with my dad in the 1940s. Dad would find us a place in the corner of the covered end halfway down the slope. He would put me on the crash barrier, like many kids of the day and then stand with his mates. Dad would also take me to the Rovers and again like many Bristolian people during those days we would alternate between both Bristol clubs. I started to go regularly to the City during the 1957–58 promotion season. I would go to games then with my mates and I would go to the very back of the covered end. I would climb five steps of terracing and then get up on the back sheeting rail of the stand so I could have a better view. I certainly needed it when we played Blackpool in the FA Cup. The crowd was over 42,000 and I have never known the covered end so packed ready to get a glimpse of Sir Stanley Matthews. Even though City had massive crowds at that time I never ever felt threatened in the terraces I suppose it was indicative of those days, perhaps supporters were different then. When I think back many things would not be allowed in todays game in particularly at half-time when ground staff would carry a bed sheet around the ground for supporters to throw coins into it as a collection for the half-time band. I was hit on the head many a time by coins raining down from the back of the stand as supporters tried to hit the sheet. And as for the toilets in the covered end, well lets not even go there. I will be sorry to see that part of the ground go, but I can see the need for change to take the club into the future.

David Woods
Bristol City Historian

3.

THE SIXTIES

The swinging sixties, as they were known would bring about huge changes in Britain as a whole. We saw the invention of the teenager and it was if there was a massive wave of optimism that had left the austere 40s and 50s in its wake. Many people describe it as if the world suddenly became full of colour. Wages had almost doubled from the 1950s with the average wage at £948 per year and a ticket to Ashton Gate costing 2s6d, which equates to 12.5p in todays money. People started to buy their own homes, cars and also the decade saw the start of the package holiday that saw people from this country venture abroad to sample different countries cultures. Fashion also appeared on the streets and surfaced on the terraces as well as youngsters started to forge their own identity. When you look back to previous decades, to suggest to the office worker in his suit and tie or the granddad in his cap and muffler, standing on the terraces in the 30s and 40s that the clothes on his back had anything to do with anything would have made you a laughing stock. Fashion was something that belonged in glossy magazines and certainly not the football terraces. Years ago supporters hurried to the match straight from work, so filled terraces with men in work attire and nobody thought anything of it. Initially, at least young people brought their fashion from the streets and onto the terracing, most obviously the boots, jeans and braces of the late 60s skinhead fashions into which the gib of your scarf or the set of your de-bobbed bobble hat could be incorporated to make your own statement. This was also the same for music as fans started to sing popular songs of the time and co-ordinate the words into songs about their club. This seemed to make the terraces more tribal and a world away from the polite clapping and cheering of the 40s and 50s. This was a real golden period for football in Britain as a whole, with Alf Ramsey's men winning the World Cup in 1966 the public became evermore thirsty for the game and footballers found themselves more and more in the limelight, advertising everything from aftershave to ice lolly's especially with the introduction of the BBC's *Match of The Day* programme where players would find themselves beamed into households all over the country on a Saturday night. The most fundamental change in the game came about with the abolition of the maximum wage that had strangled players through the previous eras. 1962 saw two radical realignments of the relationship between professional footballers and their employers. The first of the two profound changes was the abolition of the 'retain and transfer' system, an archaic clause by which-even at the end of his agreed term of contract. a players registration was retained by his club. A player could not leave one club to join another of his own volition, no matter what notice he served. Clubs 'owned' players to a degree, even in these times it was unique in employment law. After his eventual transfer from Newcastle to Arsenal George Eastham took the principle to the High Court and overturned the system that had led to a bitter and extended dispute with his former club on the expirery of his last contract. While Eastham 'freed' his fellow professionals. Jimmy Hill led the 2,000 members of the Professional Footballers Association through months of industrial dispute, eventually abolishing the maximum wage of £20 a week at the time. At Ashton Gate 1966 would see the club set about demolishing the old cowshed stand and were in the process of building a brand new stand, which was to be called the Dolman Stand after their popular chairman Harry Dolman. The structure would be finished in the 1970s at a cost of £250,000. On the pitch the club started the decade in Division Three but finished it in Division Two after promotion in the 1964–65 season. The supporters were treated to some of the clubs greatest players during this decade such as John Atyeo, who also retired amongst emotional scenes at Ashton Gate mid way through the decade and who's mark on the club will never ever diminish. Brian Clark, Mike Gibson, and Johnny Quigley to name but a few, whilst the club were managed by Fred Ford and later in the decade a young manager called Alan Dicks, who would go on and cement himself in the folklore of Bristol City fans. Bristol as a whole was on the up with not only existing industries such as the port of Bristol and the tobacco industry with its subsidiary outlets flourishing. The aircraft industry to the north of the city would also produce one of the most iconic planes of all time during this decade, The Concorde. And this with an upsurge in housing developments across the city at places like Stockwood, Whitchurch and Brislington saw Bristol as one of the up and coming city's in the uk.

I was first taken to Ashton Gate by my dad. I can't remember the exact year but it would have been early 1960s for sure and I would have been about nine or ten. Being a

Hartcliffe lad a trip to the Gate was always going to be a rite of passage for me. When I look back I'm quite proud that I was able to have such an input into the history of this part of the ground. I loved it instantly, seeing players like Mike Gibson, Jack Bonner, Tony Ford, Brian Clark and of course John Atyeo was a big thrill. After a while I started to go on my own with my mates from school and we would all go in the covered end to watch the games. Around 1967–68 I was leaving school and the whole music thing started and it was really exciting times to be a teenager. My mates and I were all into the skinhead scene wearing Doc Martin boots, Staypress trousers, Fred Perry and Crombie coats and listening to reggae, Tamla Motown and ska. We all used to meet up in a cafe on the top of Winterstoke road called Barrittos before the games. And that became the meeting point for the south Bristol lads. Inside you would have all the different mobs Knowle West, Withywood, Highridge, Hartcliffe, Bedminster, Brislington and Ashton all sharing the same goal, which was a love for Bristol City. From the cafe we would all march en masse to the ground, singing and shouting all the way. It was in the late sixties that we used to start to travel to away games and we would go all over the country. We noticed that every club we visited had a proper 'End', a place where supporters would go and show their support for their club and be singing about the end they stood in that meant so much to them. They would also sing songs from the music charts and change the words to fit their club and end. Aston Villa had the Holte End, United had the Stretford End, Liverpool The

Kop, Manchester City The Kippax so we decided that we would rename the covered and have an identity to where we stood at Ashton Gate. So we all put our heads together and for a while the covered end was called The East Bank then Stokers, due to Winterstoke Road then we decided to call it the East End as the East End of London was a rough and tough place and we could make it a rough and tough place for rival supporters to know about and for all the lads to come together, and that was about 1969 and the name has stuck ever since and grown from there. Looking back I think the sixties were a landmark in football especially from the view of the terraces, England had won the World Cup in 1966 and with fashion along with the Beatles, The Stones and black music these things made their way to the terraces and Britain seemed to come out of the drab war tainted 1950s and into an era of hope.

Angus
Bristol City terrace legend

I was taken there by my dad. The place had a magical feel about it; you felt that you were part of something, especially when they all sung. Dad would put me down the front while he stood at the back with his mates. I remember us smashing Bradford Park Avenue 6–1. The place will always remind me of my dad.

Roger Phillips
Williams stand season ticket holder

I used to meet my mates on the wall by the Winterstoke Bus depot; we would then go into the East End together. This one time they were late so I went in on my own. I must have been about 16. The end was filling up and the players were kicking the ball about before kick-off. I was watching the pitch when suddenly I heard my mates shout 'Byrney' as I turned round a ball from the pitch hit the back of my head like a cannon. It knocked me forward with such speed that I fell on top of this bloke minding his own business. The whole end roared with laughter. I was a bit shell shocked and waved away the St John Ambulance as I was too embarrassed. My mates told me later that it was John Quigley who hit me and apparently Mike Gibson the City 'keeper was in fits of laughter!

Tony Byrne
City fan who watches from the safety of the
Dolman Stand

I first went and stood in the East End when I was seven years old. My dad used to take me and put me just in front of him. I used to stand on the wall and look through the railings. I remember one game against QPR in the late 60s. I was peering through the railings when QPR forward Rodney Marsh picked up the ball and headed for the City goal as the 90 minutes approached. With the clock ticking he blasted a shot wide of Mike Gibson's goal but straight into the railings where I was stood, the force knocked me off the wall and onto the floor. With that the final whistle blew and as my dad tended to my bruised back Rodney Marsh ran over and asked my Dad if I was ok,with that he took off his shirt and gave it to me. I kept that shirt until I lost it in a house fire in 1996.

Simon Price
City and Rodney Marsh fan

My favourite memory watching City from the East End is the Oldham game in the 1964–65 season when we won promotion to the Second Division. I always went to the East End and I loved it there. On this particular afternoon the atmosphere was incredible we were jammed in like sardines. I remember when Atyeo and Clark scored for us we all just went mental. I started the game on the right side of the end and with all the jumping around and swaying I finished in the middle. We all ran on the pitch at the end to celebrate. It was a great memory.

Terry Hamblin
City fan

I was first taken to Ashton Gate on 29 August 1964. I had pestered my dad for ages to take me to a game and eventually he succumbed. 'Well go to the City' he said 'There are no Rovers in this family.' So that was it, as I recall it was a wonderful sunny day and as I was taken through the turnstile one shilling and three pence (old money) for me and two bob for dad. A programme was six pence I still have it. We were playing Walsall, it was the third match of an eventful season, City had lost the opener 5–2 at Scunthorpe and then won 5–1 at home to Barnsley on the Tuesday night. What struck me was the colour, the bright green grass, the red paint of the railings and the old tin stand where the Dolman is now. There were no player warm ups in those days they just ran out onto the pitch with a cracking version of Al Jolson's 'Red Red Robin goes.' playing over the tannoy. I was put on the railings to the left hand side of the goalposts facing the open end, with my feet through the bottom of the rails and my hands wrapped around the uprights next to my dad's mates (Mark Flicker and Steve?? I forgot his surname). The adults then got a pass out to go to the supporters club for a pint. I was also struck by the kit. Everything on the telly was black and white, so were Walsall that day. City in red shirts with a white round neck and cuffs (no shirt sleeves), white shorts and red and white socks. Walsall in a German style away kit, same pattern as City but white and black trim ,black shorts, white socks with a black top. The game began with Walsall getting an early goal, but after they were down to ten men, one unfortunate chap broke his leg (no subs in those days) Big John got hold of the game and we won 5–1. A John Atyeo hat-trick, a Tony Ford penalty and a goal from Brian Clark did the job, I was one happy nine-year-old and could not wait to come back. When I did the following week, with my seven-year-old brother Martin (his first game) I saw Workington thrashed 5–0, their fancy sky blue kit could not hold back a Brian Clark hat-trick and a double from big John. The next match was my first night game a 4–0 win over Southend United (navy with white pinstripes, white shorts and socks – very flash), Bobby 'the shadow' Williams added to another big John treble. So there we have it, first three games, not less than four goals and a hat-trick every time. One lucky boy, I was hooked who wouldn't be? Plus at the end of that season we went up in second place behind Carlisle and above Mansfield on goal average. That season we drew 1–1 at Eastville but in front of 20,000 won 2–1 against them at the Gate in mid February and went on a great run that saw the Robins only drop four points from then until that day in April when we went up. Since then, Martin and I have pretty much seen it all, ups and downs heady days and awful ones, but it's in the blood. Why else would anyone go to Carslile, Newcastle, Hull, and Mansfield etc? I have sadly developed a fascination with kits, who wears what and why due to those initial indoctrinations of sun and colour.

Phil Rollings
City fan and kit aficionado

JANTZEN DERRICK

Jantzen Derrick was truly a star in the making when he signed for his home town club in 1959. This England schoolboy international was persued for his signature by many of the games top clubs, but it was the team he had watched as a young lad with his father that was in his heart. He made his debut at Lincoln City's Sincil bank aged 16 and 324 days becoming the youngest player ever to play for Bristol City. Derrick went from strength to strength under the guidance of manager Fred Ford. As with most talented skilful players everybody had an opinion about the youngster. To some he was frustrating, beating four players then not finding the final touch. To others he was a special talent that should be looked after. Jantzen spent 12 years at City playing with such greats as John Atyeo and Brian Clark. He was released in 1971 after a brief spell on loan at Mansfield Town. He was then contacted by Paris Saint-Germain and was offered the chance to play for them in France, this he did, for a season, becoming one of the first players to venture abroad. On his return he played for Bath City and Keynsham Town. Today he still gets to City games and always gets a tremendous response from the City faithful no matter how frustrated they were by his talent.

I used to go to the City with my dad. We lived in Bedminster so it was the only club for us. We used to go to games and stand in either the open end or in front of the wooden stand that is now the Dolman Stand. My first real memory of watching games was stood in front of the stand watching City play Rovers in the 1958 FA Cup tie where Geoff Bradford scored an off side goal to win the game. I remember when I signed as an apprentice at the club we had many chores to do at the ground from sweeping the terraces, doing the kit and boots, and general painting around the ground. When it came to sweeping the terraces I always tried to get myself in the East End by the turnstiles as that's where you would have more chance of picking up a few bob that had been dropped by supporters as they came in. Perhaps they were all a bit worse for wear on arrival? When it came to playing at Ashton Gate the East End always generated the noise at the ground, it was as if the end got the whole ground going, which to us players was really special. It was the same if we managed to score in front of them as it was our supporters and they would go mad, not forgetting that if you were having a stinker of a game the East End would let you know first (and I had a few). One season sticks in my mind and it was the winter of 1962–63 which was the worst since 1948. There was heavy snowfalls which cancelled most of our games and training right up until march. To get over the training problem we used to have to do all our running up and down the East End, this went on for weeks and I was sick of the bloody place by the time the weather got better. I will miss the old East End when it goes but I suppose clubs have to move on and give supporters better facilities nowadays.

JANTZEN DERRICK
BRISTOL CITY: 1959–71
APPEARANCES: 292 (7)
GOALS: 36

BOBBY 'SHADOW' WILLIAMS

Bobby Williams was truly a Bristol City player who had the club running through his veins. A Bedminster lad who learned his trade as a youngster in the park under the shadow of Ashton Gate. He signed for the club after his dad had written to Ashton Gate asking if his son could have a trial. The club agreed and after a dazzling display in the trial match young Bobby found himself training on Tuesday and Thursday nights with the club.

After being taken on by City he worked his way through the youth team, colts, reserves and finally achieved his dream to be a first team player. Williams was a quick, skilful player with a knack of being in the box at just the right time and he became a perfect foil for City strikers such as John Atyeo and Brian Clark. He was a real fans favourite and it was a shock when he was sold to Rotherham United for £9,200 in 1965. Bobby had made 214 appearances in his beloved red shirt and scored 82 goals in the seven years he had spent with the club. After a short period with Rotherham he moved back down south to City rivals Bristol Rovers before moving on to Reading where after a short playing career he has been youth team and reserve team boss in a 30 year association with the club. At present he is a scout for Reading but his only team still to this day is Bristol City.

I have always been a lover of the covered end as I call it. When I was a kid I used to walk to Ashton Gate from my house in Bedminster and stand in the covered end. There is a whole load of memories for me in that part of the ground from when I was a kid. The promotion team of 1955 featuring John Atyeo and Cyril Williams were a great influence on me. I also remember watching us being 2–0 down against Walsall and coming back to win 3–2, the crowd erupted on the final whistle and the atmosphere was incredible. I always wanted to be a footballer and as a kid I used to play in the park near the ground although sometimes the older lads would not let me play, but I never gave up and in the end they would shout 'Here he is again, our Shadow' and that nickname came with me on to the professional game where it stuck due to the way I would apparently 'ghost' into the box. I feel so privileged to have played for City, I watched them as a boy and ended up pulling on that shirt; there are not many people who can say that. When I joined the ground staff I used to mark the pitches out and roll them on the morning of the match. Helping me were two lads Frank Jacobs and Mike Summerbee. Mike has gone on to be a good friend over the years, I always rib him about City taking me on and letting him go, he did not do too bad out of it becoming a Manchester City legend. I have great memories of my time on the ground staff with City particularly the covered or East End. It was always a race when it was time to sweep the terraces as we all wanted to get to the turnstiles where there might be a few quid knocking about that fans had dropped. I also had a few hairy moments like painting red oxide on the roof of the East End; I can't imagine clubs letting academy kids do that nowadays. And of course I remember playing in front of the end which always gave me the confidence to think that I was going to score in front of them. Like the time we beat Bristol Rovers and I hit a volley that screamed in to the top corner at that end. We won the game 4–1 and I think it was the best goal I ever scored, also the time when we beat Southend 6–3 and Barry Meyher scored Three and I got three, two of mine in front of the East End. I had some great times at City and never wanted to leave, but my time was up and Gerry Sharpe was playing well in my position so that's football although if I came back from Rotherham in the week to see friends I would contact Fred Ford to ask him to buy me back. When I signed for City all those years ago Big John Atyeo came up to me and asked what my ambitions were. I told him I wanted to play for City, Play with him, manage the club and play for England. Looking back two out of the four isn't bad going. The covered end of the ground evokes all those memories for me and that's why I will be sad to see it go. In fact I have told my wife that when I pass away I would love my ashes to be scattered at that end of the ground, that's how much it means to me.

BOBBY 'SHADOW' WILLIAMS
BRISTOL CITY: 1958–65
APPEARANCES: 214
GOALS: 82

I am really sad that the East End is going, I have always thought of it as the most iconic part of the ground, but I do realise that the game has moved on now and clubs want to provide a better environment for supporters to watch games. It has always been the part of the ground that I have watched games right from the early sixties when it was just the 'covered end'. My dad took me down to my first ever game in 1963. It was the opening game of the season against Rovers (What a game for your first one). I was completely in love with football and City as I stood in the covered end with my dad and some of his mates from work. I was eight years old and I will never forget that afternoon as City won 3–0 with goals from Atyeo, Derrick and Hooper. All the hundreds of times I have gone through those turnstiles over the years I never fail to remember that game and my first ever match stood in the East End. I will miss it when its gone

Bob Wilkinson
City fan for over 50 years

Its funny but my very first introduction to football was at Eastville, Bristol Rovers ground. I was taken there by my dad who was of that generation where they would watch City one week and Rovers the next. The lads in Rovers Tote end fascinated me. I loved their singing and chanting and too be honest I was more intrigued by that than I was with the game. I decided then that I would go to games on my own and being from Knowle West it was always going to be the red half of the city for me. The fact that City had its own end fascinated me and even in my primary school Christ The King we would go too opposite ends of the play-ground which we called the Tote end and the East End taunt each other then run at each other and try and 'Take' the other lads end fighting as we went. I don't remember my first game at Ashton Gate but I know I was around seven years old and to go in the East End on your own with your mates at that time was quite an intimidating thing but I loved it. I remember looking at the older lads who were goading and singing at rival supporters and thinking I would love to be like them. I felt as though the East End was part of me.

John 'Doddy' Dodimead
Life long City fan

Great to be able to share some memories about the East End. When I first started standing at that part of the ground it was always referred too as the covered end. I never really knew why it became the East End. But the name has always stuck. It was exciting times in the sixties with music, fashion and the emergence of the teenager. All of this seemed to manifest itself on the terraces of Britain's football teams. Me and mates would spend our Saturday mornings in the clothes shops and record shops of Bedminster then spent the afternoons on the East End watching the likes of John Atyeo, Brian Clark, Jantzen Derrick and Mike Gibson who incidentally always gave us a wave when he took his place in goal in front of the East End. After the game we would then go up to the Glen at the top of Whiteladies Road or a club in Stokes Croft called The Dug Out. They were happy Days and the East End was part of it. I will miss not seeing it anymore.

Terry Windsor
City Fan

My first game at Aston Gate was 1969 City against Norwich City. I was eight years old My dad died when I was six years old and I lived with my mum, so the prospect of her taking me to football games seemed remote. So my prayers were answered in the shape of my uncle Tommy, who was a die-hard City fan. I had shown an interest in football apparently after England's 1966 World Cup win after I received a World Cup Willie football that I proceeded to kick all around the Brislington area where I lived. Tommy seizing his chance to get another City fan in the family asked my mum if he could take me. Mum said yes and I made my way to Aston Gate and a place off too the right in the East End. I remember the game vividly with the noise, the atmosphere and the lovely green grass and seeing the contrast of City's red shirts against it made a lasting memory for me. City won 4–0 with John Galley scoring his first of two goals in the first minute. The other goals came from Danny Bartley and Alan Skirton. After the game Uncle Tommy met some of his mates and they went in Wedlock's pub across the road from the ground. Tommy sat me on the wall with lemonade and a packet of crisps as I inspected my new City rosette that he bought me. After about an hour we walked home and got some fish and chips, with Tommy asking me not to tell my mum he left me outside the pub. As I lay in bed that night I knew I was hooked on City. I continued to stand in the East End with my uncle Tommy, together we shared many highs and lows following the City. Tommy passed away in 2012 aged 80. He would be really pleased to see my story in a book about City as we shared many laughs together stood in the East End

Paul Quinn and Tommy Quinn (RIP)
City fans

I first went to see City in the 1960s with my mate's. We always stood on the East End. In the early 1960s there were less chanting and you also got a few away supporters mixed in with it, but you knew that the East End was the heartbeat of the club. It was strange times looking back, young people used to start to go instead of going with their dads and when they went on their own the East End was where they were drawn. It really did feel like an extended family.

Peter Wills
Exiled City fan living in Leeds

I was a child of the sixties and went to my first City game about 1968 with my cousin Phil. The East End was a real eye-opener for me as it was the first time I had ever seen skinheads and I was shitting myself that they were going to give me some trouble what with me being only 13. There was no trouble inside, but I rember plenty outside the ground. We started to go regular and gradually started to adopt the fashion that we saw on the terraces. My mum was appalled when I went out in my football gear of Harrington jacket, jeans, brutus button down collar shirt and Doc Martins. I certainly looked the part and wear that sort of gear today and it all started as a 13-year-old on the East End.

Pungo
City and skinhead fan

I have some great memories of the East End but unfortunately they all relate to the trouble we used to have in the late sixties. I remember when it became an 'End' and we became incredibly protective of it and Aston Gate as a whole. We would fight for our end and prove that we were harder than the visiting team. I know it sounds stupid today, but that was the general feeling of the lads in the end at that time. If there was any trouble in the end people would just move away and form a sort of hole in the crowd to let us get on with it before the police would come in and throw us out.

Micky Vaughan
City fan

I don't know if it was a different time when everybody smoked or it was an evening game and it was cold. But the East End almost breathed. I can remember as a lad going to just in front of the Williams stand and looking across at the East End. It was like a bloody great mouth opening up onto the pitch, with smoke coming out, it's a memory I will always have. When I started to go in the East End I would stand by one of the supporting pillars to the left of the goal. We loved it there cos if people came in they would look at the pillar and see that the view was not great so they would move on, so it never got really busy and became like many areas 'our spot'.

John Franks
City fan

The first game I ever went to was 1962 and my dad took me to see City against Milwall. If remember rightly it ended 2–2 and John Atyeo scored both goals for City. I had not been all that interested in football before, but I will never forget the experience. It is such a monumental change in your life, being in the East End and in amongst that many people. I remember getting off the bus at Winterstoke Road and seeing all those people. The smell of the hot dogs, it was so exciting and when Ateyo scored it felt fantastic. It's a memory that I will always think about.

Danny Giles
City fan

I choose football because it was the only thing we had to do other than hanging about on the streets. We did not get much pocket money or anything. You did not save any money for sweets, you saved it for going to the City. If we were lucky we used to sneak in. If it was a big crowd you could just get on the floor, under the turnstile and in. Or you would know a bloke on the turnstile and he would say, 'Alright over you go'. Everything was geared to going to City on the Saturday. We would talk about the mob that lived at Knowle or the mob that lived in High-ridge and how many would meet up in the East End on Saturday. You would meet lads through the football and go up the Glen with them on the Saturday night, then not see them until the next time in the East End. I would say that 90% of my mates are City fans who I have met in the East End. Schoolmates were different from football mates.

The schoolmates you spent the week with but the football mates were the ones you had the fun with.

Pete Davis
City fan for years

I must have been about 10 when I started to go to the City. We all used to go together, our little neighbourhood from Bedminster, there were older brothers and we would go with them, in a group. They would dump us down by the schoolboy enclosure and we would sneak into the East End with them. As time went on we would go straight into the East End with them, almost like a right of passage as we took our place right at the back. We would see the Bedminster boys, the Knowle and Hartcliffe Boys and the Ashton boys all coming together. I loved it on match days as we would all have a sing song and chat. They were great times.

Alan Skitson
Bedminster boy

I first went to the East End in the 1950s but things in the late 60s were insidious. There certainly wasn't one day it was fine and nasty the next, it happened slowly over time, it crept up on you. Hardly anybody was arrested at football in the 1950s but then you would see a few arrests at each game and then it became more and more. There was certainly a more aggressive attitude on the terraces in the 60s, I don't mean physically aggressive, that was left to the hooligan element, but everyone was much more volatile, more outgoing, more baiting the opposition. In the 1950s you wanted City to win but it wasn't the end of the world, but during the 60s it got to the point where your Saturday was ruined if they lost. I don't really know why. Certainly there were changes in playing styles so maybe it had something to do with player's attitudes on the pitch. I am quite a relaxed person but at 3pm on a Saturday I am like a wild man. I think my football supporting certainly changed my attitude and character, I am more aggressive now than when I was younger and I put that down to football.

John Shotten
Bristol City fan and miserable old git

Back in 1967 I was employed as a GPO telegramme messenger working shifts, including the odd Saturday afternoon. It was my misfortune to be roistered to work on the afternoon of the first game of the season, City verses Huddesfield. I had never missed a first home game of the season and I had no intention of missing this one. My dad telephoned my supervisor on the morning of the game to say that I was ill in bed and would not be coming to work (the benefit of having a dad who loved City as much as I did). That afternoon standing in a crowded East End there was the usual banter between rival fans and there was no real segregation so some Huddersfield fans took advantage of the relaxed police activities. The Huddersfield fans started to throw things and that sparked the police into action and grabbed one of them and ejected him from the ground. As he was led passed me by his collar I could not hide my amusement by grinning from ear to ear and making a mocking gesture to the poor old Yorkshire man. The next moment it was my collar being grabbed as I too was started to be marched out of the ground by two rather burly constables who each held one of my arms behind my back. As I was led around the perimeter of the pitch, who should be sitting in the main grandstand but my supervisor. From that day onwards I was referred to by him as a long haired lout but he never grassed me up. I wonder if he should have been working too.

After being warned by the police as to my future behaviour I was unceremoniously dumped in the Winterstoke Road car park where I was almost immediately approached by one of my work colleagues who was running towards the ground and obviously in a hurry. He told me he had been held up at home as his son was ill but he decided to come after all and would I like his sons seat. I told him I had just been thrown out but he said we should give it a try as he had a season ticket in the Grandstand and nobody would know. So we proceeded to go back into the ground and I sat there in one of the best seats in the ground with my Doc Marten boots and my woolly red and white scarf tucked into my braces whilst sat amongst blokes in shirts and ties.

Bill Wimble
Ex GPO worker but still a City fan

Great memories of the East End when I was a kid in the 1960s. One in particular were 1966 just after England won the World Cup. I must have been about 14 and City played Leeds United in a benefit game for John Atyeo, City lost 4–2 but Leeds brought the World Cup with them. It was magical and I could not believe that I was seeing it especially at Aston Gate.

Chris Dowdrey
City Fan

I will always remember a game from about 1963. It was against QPR and I was in the East End with my mates as usual. I also seem to remember that it was Boxing Day and it was terrible foggy, so much so that we could not see a thing. I have never ever seen fog at the city so bad. In the end they called the game off and it took me and my mates about two hours to get back home to Brislington. All the buses were stopped along with cars so we walked home.

Alan Ford
City Fan

I loved John Atyeo and I saw his entire career from the East End. He was a true gentleman on and off the field, the sort of player that would be worth millions in today's market. I particularly remember his last game for us against Ipswich Town around 1966. We won 4–1 with Bush, Parr and of course John got two. When the whistle blew I ran onto the pitch even though I was in my late twenties, I was in tears as I could not believe it was his last game for us. After the game I waited outside the players entrance for him to come out. Eventually he did and I shook his hand and thanked him for all the memories he had given me over the years he said, 'My pleasure' and I will never forget that moment as I am so pleased I got too speak to him.

Stuart Pope
Atyeo fan

Atyeo was my hero at the City. I loved the fact that he always gave 100% for the club. We used to cheer him on from the covered end. I remember at the time around 1961 there was a song in the charts by Jimmy Deans called *Big bad John* we adopted it and sang it to him all the time, in fact it lasted throughout the rest of his career. He would always smile when he came up for a corner attacking the covered end as we sang. One game that always sticks in my mind was the 1965 game against Oldham when we clinched promotion. There was about 30,000 packed into Ashton Gate and you could not move in the covered end. I think I started at the back and ended up away to the left. You just got pushed along like a sea it was both scary and exciting looking back. City won the game 2–0 with John and Brian Clark getting the goals to clinch promotion to Division Two. I remember it as a fantastic day for all connected with the club especially the supporters.

Bob Kelly
City fan

I have some great memories of watching various City teams from the East End over the years. I loved that part of the ground. It was the very first place I saw my beloved Bristol City from. I was a young lad of six years old when my dad took me from our home in Whitchurch to Ashton Gate. We went on the bus and it was a real adventure for me. Looking back I was just excited to spend a day with my dad who at the time, like many fathers always seemed to be in work. The game was City against Northampton in the 1961 season. City won the game 1–0 with John Atyeo getting City's goal. I loved the atmosphere and was enthralled by the game as I stood with some other children at the front of the covered end as all the dads were stood together behind us. After the game I asked my dad who the number 10 was? He seemed surprised, as I wasn't asking about John Atyeo but Brian Clark. Dad explained to me that he had just started playing for the club and how his dad used to play for City before him. Right from that moment Brian Clark was my favourite player. I would always be Clarky when we played football in the fields or in the playground.

My lasting memory was when a group of us had ridden our bikes from Whitchurch to Ashton Court in the summer. As we went passed the City ground there was a couple of players kicking a ball against the wall of the covered end in the car park. We raced over and incredibly one of them was Brian Clark training with a few others in his pre season. He chatted to us and he let us kick the ball to him and he passed it back, I genuinely thought I was going to pass out in excitememnt. after about 20 minutes the players went back inside Ashton Gate but they gave us lads a moment that we cherished forever. I always followed Brian's career, even when he left us for other clubs and when he passed away a few years ago I went to the church in Cardiff where his funeral was taking place and I stood outside the Gate with my City scarf on and applauded with everyone else as they brought his coffin inside. I said a small prayer for a man who gave a group of scruffy ten year olds his time and I will never forget that. I thank you for letting me share that moment with you.

Johnny Willerd
RIP Brian Clark (legend)

I used to be a police officer in the 60s and I would always put my name down for some overtime in the shape of working at Ashton Gate on a Saturday afternoon. I lived in Whitchurch and was based in Bedminster. The crowd was no trouble most of the time. We were based in front of the East End and we would walk up and down the perimeter of the pitch until they kicked off making sure nobody ran on. Five minutes before the half-time whistle we would do it again and also five minutes before the game ended. I think the way the police acted reflected the way society acted They mirrored each other. In the 50s and 60s Police were very good-natured. We would stand there take a bit of stick from the fans and have a joke back, we would also pass kids down to the front but in the 70s it all got a bit nasty and the police and certain elements of supporters became real enemies' I loved my time at the City. I would ride my bike back to Whitchurch and be home for tea after the game. I loved my time in front of the East End.

Michael Woodridge

In todays world of footballs giant 'keepers Mike Gibson would probably never have got to pull on a professional shirt let alone become one of Bristol City legendary players and arguably their greatest 'keeper of all time. Standing 5ft 9ins tall what Gibson lacked in height he more than made up for in bravery and timing, two commodities that would win over the Ashton Gate faithful. Signed from Shrewsbury Town for £5,000 by City manager Fred Ford, the Derby born Gibson became the perfect replacement for ageing City 'keeper Tony Cook in the 1962–63 season. Gibson would go from strength to strength between the the City uprights showing bravery, timing and an ability to stop shots like no other the Robins had ever seen. A stalwart of the promotion team in the 1964–65 season Gibson would spend 10 seasons at the club becoming a favourite with fans. Injury and the emergence of up and coming local lad Ray Cashley would see Gibson leave the club in 1972 and head for Gillingham where he would go on to win another promotion with the Kent side. A return to Bristol City in a scouting capacity would arrive on his retirement from football and also lead to work with City's youth team and reserves, a job he would do alongside his new occupation as a postman around Bristol. Retired today Gibson can still be seen around Ashton Gate on match days, where he never fails to get a fantastic reception from those fans he stood in front of all those years ago.

MIKE GIBSON

I was signed from Shrewsbury Town in 1962 as replacement for Tony Cook. Apparently Tony was getting on in age and was struggling with injury, so the City Manager was after a replacement. Fred came to see me in a game for Shrewsbury against Peterborough United and I had a stormer, nothing got passed me. Next thing I know Shrewsbury had agreed a £5,000 fee and I was off. I knew nothing of Bristol to be honest but I loved it the moment I arrived. I think I made my debut against Crystal Palace towards the end of the 62–63 season at Ashton Gate in a 1–1 draw and the covered end gave me a fantastic reception as I ran towards them. I had a great rapport over the years with the City supporters at that end of the ground. I always used to mark out four paces from the goal line then make a mark in the ground so I would not loose my bearings positional I would then finish this off with a jump up and touch the crossbar. The fans would count with me then give up a mighty cheer when I touched the bar it was brilliant and made me feel ten foot tall to have that kind of support behind me. I used to see the same people behind the goal every home game as everyone had their own pitch behind the goal. I would have a chat with a few before the game and I would laugh to myself at some of the comments they would shout during the game at the opposition. I had some great memories at City mainly the promotion year of 1964–65 and also the League Cup semi-final first leg against Spurs in 1970–71. We drew 1–1 and it was a fantastic night although we lost 2–0 after extra-time in the second leg. To be that close to Wembley was very hard to take and it would have been a wonderful

*end to my time at City. It was a difficult thing to leave the
club but Ray Cashley was coming through and playing fantastic so it was only a matter of time. I went to Gillingham and
won promotion with them but my heart was always with City,
as I loved the area. I was invited to get back involved with
the club by the then boss Terry Cooper and I worked with the
youths and reserves, which I loved. I still go to games and I
am delighted to get a great reception from the fans. I had some
wonderful times in front of the East End and I will never forget
it. It was a privilege to stand in front of them week in week
out. I will be sad to see the old stand go but I think the club are
on the way up and the new stand will be a wonderful addition
to Aston Gate.*

MIKE GIBSON
BRISTOL CITY: 1962–72
APPEARENCES: 376

I first went to see City in the 1960s and we always stood
in the East End, as it became known. I used to go with my
mates from Hartcliffe where we lived and we would get to
North Street about 12pm and go into a coffee house called
Greco's, which had a jukebox that played all our favourite
records. I used to work in a garage in Brislington in the
week and I hated getting up for work but on Saturdays
when it was match days I couldn't wait to get up and meet
my mates. We stood on the terraces and sang all game.
My favourite player was Brian Clark, he looked like a film
star and always said hello if we saw him before or after the
game. My favourite game would have to be a home game

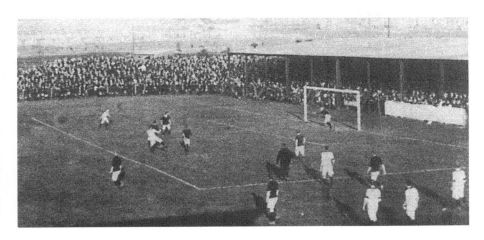

A 21,000 crowd see Bristol City lose 2–1 at the hands of Manchester United in 1906. The game was City's first ever match in the top flight. The picture clearly shows the original covered end that was demolished and rebuilt in 1928.

Bristol City v Romford in the FA Cup 1st Round 1932. A view from the open end gives an indication of how packed the covered end was in this 4–0 win for City.

*A page from the Bristol Evening Post Newspaper 1935 showing
Bristol City's famous FA Cup game against Portsmouth. The crowd
inside Ashton Gate that day was rumoured to have been around
50,000. Note the fans on the covered end roof.*

Bristol City Reserves against Bristol Rovers Reserves in the 1950s. A view from the open end of the Cowshed, now the Dolman stand.

Bristol City v Oldham Athletic 1964–65 season. John Atyeo, out of picture, scores City's second in front of the East End to clinch promotion in front of 28,248 at Ashton Gate.

Above: Aerial shot of Ashton Gate and surrounding area circa 1968.

Left: City's new floodlights going in between the East End and the Williams, in December 1965.

Donnie Gillies celebrates in front of the East End in the 1970s.

From the cauldron of the East End before the bulldozers moved in.

The East End from the Williams stand.

The East End with seats, days before the bulldozers moved in.

With the East End removed the builders can pile drive the steel work ready for the new structure.

The new stand takes shape.

The view from the Atyeo Stand of the new structure.

The future of Ashton Gate.

with Barnsley when we won 5–1 and Clarky got a hat-trick. I think we all celebrated in the Glen nightclub up in Clifton afterwards. They were brilliant days. Although I have supported City through the eras I have to say the 60s were my favourite.

Peter Hall
City fan living in Bath

My fondest memories of supporting Bristol City are in the 1960s. I got my first car which was a Hillman Imp. It was my pride and joy. I worked at John Hall glass in Hengrove and every Saturday I would clean my car then travel to Ashton Gate with my brother Terry. We would park on Raleigh road and have a couple of pints in North Street before standing in the East End and watching City. I remember their were more younger people in the East End at that time, probably lads who had gone to the City with their dads in the 1950s and they now felt they wanted to go alone and the East End seemed the perfect place for us to congregate in those days. I think that's why there is so much affection for that part of the ground as opposed to other parts. I know it sounds cheesy but I felt like there was a real family in there, I made so many friends standing in that part of the ground who I still see today. My favourite games were always against the Rovers. Where I worked you were either red or blue there was none of this supporting teams from another city it always depended where you lived or who your dad supported. I remember City beating the gas 5–0 around 1969 in the Gloucester cup. It was a great night and chanting was just starting on the terraces and the whole of the East End were singing Easy, Easy, I could not wait to get into work the next day so I could give the Rovers fans some stick. It was all light hearted but a wonderful time. Many thanks for letting me share my thoughts for this book.

Peter Windsor
Exiled City fan living in Taunton

I heard that Bristol City were doing a book about memories of the covered end so here is mine. I'm glad the club have acknowledged how much that crappy old end meant to people over the years. The smell of the cigarettes, the hot dogs, and even the appalling smell of the open toilets wafting across the terrace mean a lot to me. I first started to stand on the end in the early sixties with my dad. He would stand with his mates and I would be moved like a lot of kids in those days to the front right behind the goal. I loved going with my dad as I never really saw a lot of him during the week and I think it was the same for lots of kids in those days, Saturdays meant I got to be with him most of the day. I loved seeing him with his mates at the games he was a different kind of person; as though all the responsibilities were gone he would laugh and tell jokes and have the rest of the pub in fits of laughter. He was a bit more sensible when he was home. I will always remember watching John Galley play, he was my favourite player at the time and looking back I think he is my favourite City player of all time. I was a bit too young for John Atyeo and Galley certainly fitted the bill. I particularly remember two goals he scored against Oxford United around 1968. Everybody pushed towards the front when he scored the first and I got crushed against the barrier. Word got back to dad who was at the back of the covered end and he came down and saw me upset so he picked me up and I watched the rest of the game from his shoulders. Dad talked to me the whole game like a football commentator and when Galley got the second I thought I was going to hit my head on the roof he jumped so high. We got chips on the way home as usual. I ate mine still on my dads shoulders it's a memory I will always remember. So as they pull the covered end down I am very excited that I may have my memory about a Saturday afternoon with my dad in the book. He would have loved it

Jimmy Skuse

I loved standing on the East End. I first started going in the sixties and I continued right up until they put the seats in and then I went over to the Atyeo stand. I like the fact that the club are acknowledging the East End before they take it down. There is one thing that I wont miss and that will be the toilets. I swear if I go to a game on a Saturday the smell of the urinals stays with me until around Tuesday lunchtime. Like a lot of people I have seen some great teams and some great players grace the Ashton Gate pitch over the years, so when I heard this book being promoted on the radio I sat and thought long and hard about writing in. The one game that stays in my mind was 1966–67 season and it was John Atyeos benefit game against Leeds United. I remember Leeds brought the World Cup with them and for a young 12-year-old like myself it was magical. I knew John Atyeo was a special player even at that age and I remember my dad telling me 'We wont see his like again. Remember this day son'. I think we lost 4–2 but it's a memory I will always have and I hope its good enough for you to put it in the book.

Sam Foley
City fan, Filton

Bristol City's covered end always makes me think of my childhood. I was brought up in Ashton through the 1960s and the ground was a magnet to us kids in the area, not just on match days but also especially in the summer holidays. We would get into the ground some days and watch the first team training on the pitch now and then. The club knew we were there but they never cared in those days. We would look out for our idols like John Atyeo and Brian Clark and fair play to them they would always give us a wave when we called out there names. Players have certainly changed over the years. Now the club have security people at the training ground. Another summer activity for us would be to play football non-stop on the ground behind the covered end and we would all dream of scoring for the City. I remember games going on until late into the night and then I would see the shadowy figure of my mum in the distance and I knew it was time to go home for tea. There would be about 20 kids all playing around the ground and nobody ever moved us on. I suppose it just shows how times of changed. So I will have mixed emotions when the covered end is pulled down, it will be a little part of my childhood that will disappear under the rubble, but as a lifelong Bristol City fan I am pleased the club are moving forward with a state of the art facility for the fans.

Mike Potter
Exiled City fan living in Exeter

I found out that this book was being done whilst listening to Radio Bristol. Being a lifelong City fan I thought what a great idea for the club to acknowledge the fans who stood through the eras in the covered end, East End and Wedlock stand. I have always stood in the East End when I started to go to games on my own, which would have been in the seventies onwards. My memories of the East End are, I imagine the same of everybody else's in those days of atmosphere, noise and although the place had a very dark and violent reputation with rival fans, for us City fans it was a place were you felt safe and together with your mates. For my memory I must tell you about the times I would go to the City in the 1960s. My dad was a member of the St John Ambulance brigade and he would attend City games through the season doing what is a very worthwhile roll. Round about 1964 he decided that I would join the Brigade along with him and do my bit at games along with other events across the City. I was 12 at the time and music and fashion were starting to take off with me, not forgetting girls. My dad was not a man who accepted the word no. So off I go to pass the exams and suddenly I am issued with this God awful uniform with a white sash and even worse a hat that made me look like a bus conductor. Now no offense to bus conductors but in 1964 that was not the look a lad who was approaching his teens was looking for. Excitedly dad informed me that we would be attending City games together in our roll with the service.

We walked out around the pitch with the other volunteers and I knew we were heading for the East End. There was a small wooden bench that we sat down on. The walk to that bench and the following 90 minutes against Barnsley even today brings me out in a sweat. I just wished the ground could open up and swallow me whole. I have never been so embarrassed, the uniform did not fit and I felt a right plonker as all the 'cool' lads shouted abuse and generally took the piss at my expense. My dad was oblivious to the shouts coming from behind him. I continued to go with dad even though I hated every minute of it and I plucked up the courage to tell him at the end of that season that I did not see myself progressing in the St John Ambulance service. He was shocked but we negotiated that I would go to Air Cadets instead which I agreed. Towards the end of the 1960s I started to go to the East End on Saturdays with my mates. I would still see dad at the games but he had moved to in front of the Williams Stand. So there is a part of me that will miss the old East End when it is knocked down but hopefully the fact that it will be removed will help erase the scare of that 1964–65 season for ever. By the way, I went to Air Cadets for three weeks before I was thrown out for fighting. I never told dad.

Andrew Somerton
Bristol City fan

I have been going to see the City from 1963 when I was about seven years old. I first went with my father and uncles who were all City fans so there was only ever going to be one team for me. Over the years I have followed City home and away and in the early years I was there at the very beginning of the East End and the start of the football violence that engulfed our game during the late 60s, 70s and 80s. My first ever game was as I said with my dad and uncles and it was Boxing day 1963 against QPR. City were knocking on the door of promotion from the Second Division and had a fantastic forward line of John Atyeo, Brian Clark, 'Shadow' Williams, Janzen Derrick and Peter Hooper. They were beating QPR 3–0 at half-time but after the break the ref came out on the centre spot and saw the fog coming across Ashton Park and called the game off. The crowd went mental and I remember the boos and shouts ringing around the East End as he gave his decision. Another early memory I have of being in the East End was at half-time four men would carry a tin bath around the ground with a big sheet and fans would throw coins into it. The collection was called 'The Lord Mayors Appeal'. The money collected would be given to local charities. There would be a small army of young lads that would pick up any coins that missed the bath and went on the pitch. Looking back it really was a Health and Safety nightmare by todays standards, how somebody never got injured I don't know. As the 60s evolved so did the grouping of supporters and the idea of a club having there own end that rival supporters would try to take. The East End would have various lads going week in and week out but they all came together on an away day at Sunderland. City drew Sunderland in the Cup and the club put on a train that left Bristol at midnight stopping at various points across the city on its way. It arrived at 6am in the morning and although the club lost 6–1 it was the start of various faces coming together as one to form a type of 'Firm'. At that time the roughest 'Mobs' that were around in the Second Division were Birmingham City who always ended up having trouble in Weston-Super-Mare after a City game and although it pains me to say it Cardiff City had a fearsome reputation. I remember some massive battles in the end as clubs like this would try and 'Take' the East End. We would always meet up in the Rising Sun pub which was run by Pete and Glynis Cox or the Coopers Arms. as we prepared for the forthcoming game listening to Desmond Dekker or Harry J and the All-stars and other reggae tunes. The name of the East End was formed after a meeting in the Marisa Café at the top of Winterstoke Road. All the lads met up and wanted to give the covered end a name and there were various suggestions like The Stokers but somebody said lets call it the East End after the East End of London which has a tough reputation and the name stuck. What helped was in 1969 City beat Rovers 5–0 and 'EAST END RULES' was sprayed all over the Tote end. The relationship with Rovers is interesting as City fans from the south of Bristol were all into the Who and the mod culture but Rovers fans seemed to be greasers and hells angels so there was a difference in us socially, even though we lived in the same city, I'm not saying all of the rovers fans were like that but all the ones I came across were. The East End at that time really was the start of something massive.

Tom Hopegood
City fan

114

4.

THE SEVENTIES

The 1970s will always be remembered as a decade of turmoil. A decade where conservative and Labour governments took on the nations unions and invariably lost. Edward Heaths Conservative government came to power in 1970 and the country suffered at the hands of a world oil crisis, a financial crash and a second miners strike in two years. Labours government led by Jim Callaghan came to power in 1974 and again the country had to deal with strikes, a three-day week caused by an energy crisis and a strangulation of the country by the relevant power industries unions and too add insult to injury inflation hit 30% leading to a humiliating bail out of the country by the International Monetary Fund, a decision that ultimately cost the Labour government its power to the Conservatives in the 1979 election. Leading the way for Britain's first female Prime Minister in the shape of Margret Thatcher. Looking back on the decade it's remarkable to see the rise of women in those times. Here we were with a female Prime Minister and yet at the start of the decade women could not even get a mortgage by themselves, in fact in 1971 the Wimpy chain of Burger restaurants would not allow single females into their restaurants after midnight on the grounds that any women on their own at that time was obviously a prostitute. Thatcher was determined that she would never

be strangled by the unions as Heath and Callaghan had been
before her and she would take the country into a very different
direction. In a backdrop to the political fighting of Government
and unions you also had weaving through these difficult times
was the troubles of Northern Ireland and the mainland bombing
campaign of the IRA. During the decade 1,173 civilians would
lose their lives as a result of the conflict on both sides of the
water. Locally Bristol was like many cities throughout the UK, it
was in the process of redevelopment albeit a very slow process
at that. W.D. and W.H. Wills opened the largest manufacturing
plant at Hartcliffe in 1974. Planers believed that this modern,
efficient, state of the art factory would produce cigarettes for
years too come. Unfortunately this would only last until 1990.
The off shoot of the move away from Bedminster would be that
this part of Bristol would have the heart ripped out of it in terms
of employment and most notably local traders in the North
Street and West Street areas would see their very lifeblood i.e.
the Wills workforce move miles away. That decision by Wills
would take the area years to regenerate itself and in some areas
that regeneration is still to happen. Wages in the city would be
the national average of £1,801 per year while it cost 8s = 40p to
see Bristol City. In the media the music of the 1970s will always
be portrayed as Slade, Abba, and the Bay City Rollers the music
of the terraces was ska, reggae, soul and towards the end of the
decade punk. As with the sixties, street fashion found its way
onto the terraces with the skinhead look of Ben Sherman shirts,
Doctor Martin boots along with Butchers coats that were taken
from the Stanley Kubricks Film a Clockwork Orange based on
the Anthony Burgess novel. The film depicts gang culture, gang
violence and it struck a chord with many fans who would copy

the fashion onto the terraces. Many of the terrace supporters would also find themselves in local clubs such as Scamps, Maxims, bailys, Broads, Tiffany's and the Locarno. With the black clouds of football violence running through the decade City's East End became a very intimidating place for some and a real spiritual home for others. There was tragedy off the pitch as Mr Bristol City, Harry Dolman passed away in 1977 aged 80. On the pitch the club gained success, and the decade would represent one of City's greatest as a team. They were mainly unknowns from other clubs sprinkled with local lads and fashioned by new manager Alan Dicks into a team that many supporters could name even today. With Dicks at the helm City would pull off one of the great FA Cup shocks in 1973–4 season as they beat the mighty Leeds United who were littered with internationals at Elland Road 1–0 after the first game drew 1–1 at Ashton Gate. City's reward would be a home tie with Liverpool who they unfortunately lost to 1–0. The club and its supporters certainly had a taste for the big time and they would be rewarded in 1976 when they found themselves amongst the country's footballing elite as they gained promotion to the First Division. Ashton Gate would be host to some of the biggest teams of the day such as Manchester united, Liverpool, Leeds United and Arsenal along with some of the games great players. And it would be to City's credit that they would hold their own in the top flight for four seasons before finally being relegated in the 1979–80 season. What is amazing about the era is that people remember the power cuts and the strikes yet they have surprisingly great affection for the decade that taste forgot. As for City fans it was certainly a golden decade.

Many things stand out regarding the East End but one in particular, me and my mate David Hughes, had just gained entry by slipping half a crown each to a guy on the Gate (by the old toilet block). I had just bought myself a crunchie bar and walked on into our favourite spot which was just to the right of the goal facing the open end (now the Atyeo stand). I was very loud in those days, the game started against Crystal Palace and when Alan Whittle (for those of you who don't remember him he always wore white boots and had a mop of white hair) was on the ball. I yelled 'Whittle is a wanker', I was just about to eat my crunchie when I was set on by three burly coppers who ejected me from the ground! Those three coppers would have a field day today with the language used on the terraces today.

Simon Ogston
Season Ticket holder in the Dolman Stand

I remember I started going to the East End with my dad when I was six back in 1979. I had to stand on a milk crate to see.

Simon Bruford
City fan

I can't believe it is the end of the East End. I can imagine the demolition team being met by a huge gathering of fans singing

1,2,3,4,5 if you want to stay alive
KEEP OF THE EAST END!

My brother says they are selling East End seats for a tenner. I'm not interested, I prefer to remember the standing crowd surges after goals in the 1970s. My favourite goal watching from the East End was Jimmy Mann's 40 yarder against one of the world's best goalies, Peter Shilton, when with Nottingham Forest in the old Division One days. I was right in line and followed the shot as it flew into the top corner. It was unstoppable. I also remember the joy of hugging strangers after the play-off win against Hartlepool and accidently knocking the glasses off a Manchester United fan while leaping around after Chris Garland's goal. He must have been a Man United fan, as he did not seem that excited. I also loved the songs of the seventies.

'Hit him on the head
Hit him on the head
Hit him on the head with a baseball bat
On the head, on the head!!'

East End Col
City Fan

Something I remember from the early 70s was going with a few friends from school and getting there early to get a space on the raised concrete at the back of the East End (right hand side looking at the pitch), which gave a great view of the game as we were not that tall! It was probably not that safe to stand there thinking about that now but at the time it was the place to be.

Nigel Bateman

When I was a kid I used to love being in my dad's Ford Cortina as we drove up from our home in Clevedon for a night game. As soon as I could see the floodlights my heart skipped a beat. We used to go in the Dolman Stand but always was transfixed by the East End and the noise it made. I used to think that when I'm older I will go there. In the eighties I moved to the East End and experienced highs, lows, danger and fear. . . and that was just from my fellow City fans.

Peter Walsh
Williams stand

Saturday 24 April 1976 a date that will live long in the memories of us 'more seasoned' Robins. City v Nott's County, last match of the 1975–76 seasons, with automatic promotion already guaranteed after victory over Portsmouth the previous match. Me and three mates head off to the Gate for a party! We cheered and sang I waved the scarf that my Nan had knitted me.

County won that day 2–1 but the result was immaterial- we were heading to the delights of the First Division (in those days the First Division meant the First Division not Division Three like nowadays). The final whistle blew, a signal for the match to end, but more importantly for the fans a chance to take their rightful place on the hallowed turf. I was 16, in the prime of my youth, and I was a country boy, used to climbing trees. . . at least I should have been. Tree climbing always looked like too much hard work when my friends scaled their dizzy heights, and I had ripped more pairs of jeans and cords climbing over barbed wire fences! So, when faced with the old spiked railings that used to adorn the East End, my dear friends upped and leapt over it like gazelles, leaving me stranded on the terrace side in a virtual prison. The team came out lead by manager Alan Dicks and captain Geoff Merrick, for the celebrations. Yes, I joined in the cheering, but it was bittersweet, I should have been on the pitch. Added to that, and remembering that mobile phones were the thing of science fiction and Tomorrows world. I had no way of finding my friends. I never did learn to climb trees.

Steve Harris
Now living in Edinburgh, but City till I die

When I was in school the East End was the place to be especially if you wanted a bit of kudos with your mates. I was 14 and when I went to the City I would go with my dad and we went to the nice safe Williams stand (This was the 70s remember). But I had always wanted to pluck up the courage to go in the East End where some of my more naughtier mates were. One Friday at school we all decided that we were all going in the East End. I told my dad and he was not too keen as it had a bit of a reputation but nevertheless he let me go on my own.

The game was 1973 against Cardiff City. So there was a packed East End singing and shouting against our Welsh Rivals. I couldn't see much of the game due to the crowd, but about 10 minutes after kick-off somebody near me threw a bottle of piss in the air and it hit a coppers back. With that two members of Avon and Somerset's finest barged their way through the packed crowd and got nearer and nearer. Suddenly they grabbed my arm and dragged me out of the ground whilst also giving me a kick up the arse telling me to go home and count myself lucky I was not arrested, I pleaded my innocence but they were in no mood to listen.

I walked home upset and in a state of shock. When I got home my mum asked me why I was home before the game, to which I replied that there was trouble so I came home. She made me a cup of tea and told me what a good lad I was. At school on the Monday I had gained legendary status amongst my peers for throwing a bottle of piss at a copper and getting thrown out like a proper hooligan. I never did tell them it wasn't me until now!!

Jimmy (Nubber) Nicholls
Ex East End hard man...For one game only!!

I remember being about eight years old and watching the City play against Middlesborough, I think it was 1971. Usually my dad and my two brothers stood in the open end complete with stools, scarfs and rattles. I am not sure why we went to the East End that day. I can remember that sometimes if other teams fans had a reputation for trouble we used to go to the 'safety' of the East End. The game sticks in my mind because I can remember Gerry Sharpe attacking the goal from the left and hearing the 'crack' of his leg breaking in a tackle. I knew it was broke because dad told me! I am now in my 50s and very much an exiled fan in Northampton, my dad is 83 and is a season ticket holder up in the Dolman stand along with my brother Phillip, his son Sam aged 21 and sometimes my elder brother Martin. I work as a golf professional and teach golf every weekend in Northampton. Still I love my Saturdays and with modern technology I can still follow the City.

Adrian Clifford
Come on you reds!!!

My dad was always a regular in the East End from the 1950s right through to the early 1990s when he passed away. At his funeral we got the hearse to take a detour into the car park behind the East End where it stopped for a minute then moved on. For me that was the most upsetting part of the Funeral. I still think of that moment today.

Mike Addidge
City fan for over 40 years

To the tune of teddy bears picnic:

> *'If you go down to the woods today,*
> *you're sure of a big surprise*
> *If you go down to the woods today you'll*

never believe your eyes
Cos Jer-emy the sugar puff bear has bought
some boots and cropped his hair
And gone to join the East End boot boys'

Andy Forster
City fan

There has been many lasting memories of the East End in the 1970s that stand out for me, obviously the night we won promotion against Portsmouth in 1976 was a wonderful night. I also remember seeing England under-21s beat East Germany 3–1 in 1971 with a youngster called Kevin Keegan in the England side. But a rain swept October evening in 1973 is my favourite. It was the night our 'keeper Ray Cashley scored from a goal-kick. The East End was packed and when Ray let fly we just watched it go on and on and on until it went over the Hull City 'keepers head. There was silence around the ground for a couple of seconds, as I don't think the ref knew what to do. In the end he gave the goal and we just went mental. We beat Hull 3–1 and on the way out of the ground I found a £10 note on the floor. I quickly picked it up and ran all the way home and gave it to my mum.

Simon Price
City fan for over 40 years

Playing Liverpool in the league cup around 74–75 season and I was 13 years old. Liverpool had a great team full of stars You could not move in the East End that night I think the crowd was 25,000. It was a fantastic atmosphere although due to the fact that we were crammed in I could only see bits of the game. The match ended 0–0 and we waited around the player's entrance after the game to see the Liverpool team before they got on their coach. I remember being thrilled when Bill Shankley signed my programme, which I still have today.

Mike Tanner
Williams stand regular

I had some fantastic times in the East End during the 1970s. The atmosphere that it generated seemed to travel all around the ground. My mates and I would congregate at the back of the end and we would have the odd youngster sat on a wall as look out for when any rival supporters were spotted. And when they were, you can imagine the East End reception we gave them. When I look back now it was a real intimidating place for some people but no different to any end up and down the country, the violence thing was certainly indicative of football at that time. Our short skinhead hair had now been replaced with either suede heads which was just a bit longer or the Rod Stewart type hair along with big flares and check jackets. You Would also get the odd long white Butchers coat worn as some sign of toughness but this came from East London clubs such as Millwall or Charlton Athletic, but it never really took off with us. We would all meet up in the Rising Sun pub across the road from the park and march all the way round the ground to the East End. After the game we would end up in Top Rank, Locarno or some other Bristol nightclub we had some great times. I saw some great games in the seventies especially the Promotion year. One that sticks in my mind was when we beat Liverpool 2–1 in 1977. Chris Garland got the two goals and the atmosphere that game was fantastic. After all this was one of Britain's greatest sides that went onto win the European Cup and we had just beat them, it was a game I will never forget.

Angus
City Terrace Legend

BRYAN DRYSDALE

In every successful side you have to have a mixture of stars and workhorses. The stars will get the plaudits and nine times out of ten will be the supporters favourites, but the work horses will be the ones who make the team work, who go and win the ball and never give up. Many successful teams over the years have had them and in the 1976 promotion team Bristol City's was full-back Brian Drysdale. The £10,000 that City paid Hartlepool in 1969 was one of the best deals they have ever done. Although he had spent the majority of his career in lower leagues 26 year old Drysdale fitted into life at City without any problems. This Mr Dependable did not miss a match for more than three seasons in the heart of city's defence. Brian had skill, speed and was a ferocious tackler who read the game like nobody else. He would put supporters on the very edge of their seats with one of his forward runs and his crossing with his famous left foot was phenomenal. Although becoming an integral part of the famous promotion team Brian would, after only a couple of games in the top flight become surplus to requirements after City signed former Leeds United and England defender Norman Hunter to bolster their defence. The move forced former centre-back and captain Geoff Merrick across the back four into Brian's position. Drysdale was loaned out to Reading and eventually left City for Oxford United and eventually moved to local amateur football, but supporters will never forget his contribution to Bristol City's most successful team.

I have always enjoyed a good relationship with the City fan that's why I never left the area when I moved clubs. I remember before I signed some of the Hartlepool lads were giving me stick about being in the back and beyond and the only thing I knew about Bristol City was that they had a 'Boy wonder' at the club called Jantzen Derrick. The moment I arrived everything just clicked for me. We had some good players and you could see that manager Alan Dicks was building something special. Alan believed in us all working and socialising together, we certainly did that. The East End is very dear to me, I used to love defending it and it really did feel like those supporters were an extra defender helping to keep the ball out and when we attacked it they made you feel like they were sucking the ball towards the net, I don't think they realise how important they were to us with their singing and chanting. Over the years they have given me many great memories. Obviously I will never forget the promotion night when we beat Portsmouth 1–0 to get to Division One. I don't think I have ever experienced tension and atmosphere like that warm evening and the relief when we did it was shared around the ground, but I will never forget the East End never stopped singing all game. Another game that sticks in my mind that year was when we beat Oldham at home 1–0 with a Paul Cheesley goal and we went on a run of about 11 games and it was that run that took us to promotion. We got a real sense that we could do it and the atmosphere that was created by the fans and in particularly the East End is always mentioned when the team get together nowadays. Obviously it is well documented how I left the club but I never really felt any animosity towards anybody at the club in fact I just feel proud to have been in that team and remembered by supporters.

BRIAN DRYSDALE
BRISTOL CITY: 1969–77
APPEARANCES: 328
GOALS: 4

There was always a really good atmosphere in the East End. I loved the singing and the noise the place made was remarkable considering it wasn't that big. One game I remember was in the seventies when we played Hull City. Billy Bremner the ex Leeds United legend was playing for Hull and when he came back in front of the East End to defend a corner we all started singing 'Fatty Fatty Bremner'. When Hull got the ball up field he turned to us and rubbed his stomach and laughed, I will always remember that.

John Wayland
City fan

The East End was a tough old place in the seventies, it was where the City lads used to hang out and if rival supporters wanted a fight, well they knew where to find them. I always went in the East End but not at the back where the hard nuts went. I was always down the front shouting and singing. Everybody talks about how the atmosphere was and in the seventies it could be really hostile. I remember one game against Cardiff City in 1972, it was Boxing Day and I went with some mates from school. I was 14 and there was some trouble in the Dolman Stand, which led to the police escorting three Cardiff fans out of the ground. The police brought them right in front of the East End for some strange reason and as expected the crowd went mental. They all started hurling objects at the Cardiff fans and the police as they walked past. Suddenly my mate Tony shouted at me, 'Baggy your head'. Unbeknown to me a dart had hit me in the back of the head and was sticking out through my hair. I panicked and pulled it out causing it to start to bleed. I let one of the St John ambulance blokes know and they treated me. I never told my parents it was a dart that hit me I just told them I fell over. But in school after the Xmas holidays I had never been so popular telling kids how I had been hit by a dart. In fact I think I told them Cardiff fans had done it.

Alan Bagshaw
East End regular until the seats

As far as I am concerned this really was a golden time for the East End. I know it was a real intimidating place in the seventies due to the violence, but to be in amongst it was a real buzz. I remember we used to go to the ground and get one of the bigger lads to bend some of the metal work at the back of the end and hey presto us young lads would all run in without paying. I used to get involved in all sorts of trouble back then. There was a certain hierarchy in amongst the East Enders and as I was only a young kid it was my job to climb up to the top of the gap at the back of the stand and act as look out for the rival fans when they tried to get in the end and take it. The real naughty fans such as Milwall, Spurs, Portsmouth would wait until 3pm kick-off to make their move, after all anybody could take an end around 1.30 pm as there was nobody in it. I would shout out 'Their coming,' and let the lads know how many in their party. It was mental looking back but I really did make friends for life. Another memory I have of the East End was me and a few mates played for local club Knowle United. As a club we never had a pot to piss in. So we decided to turn up at Ashton Gate and sweep the terraces for the club in the hope that they would give us some money too buy stuff for the club. The club let us sweep them and it was bloody hard work. We loved being in our beloved East End when nobody was about, we were singing and scratching our names in anything we could. The club gave us some programmes for doing the work but we did not care as we found £20 on the floor of the East End which back around 1975 was a lot of money. We were buzzing and bought a leather football, breakfast in the local café and lived like kings for the day. Throughout the seventies the East End became a legendary place for the City fans, and City had some fantastic games where full houses were a regular thing. I remember the atmosphere of the big games like Leeds United, Liverpool in the First Division and of course the night we got there against Portsmouth, I think the whole of south Bristol were on the pitch that night. I certainly was no saint following City in the seventies but the club and particularly the East End will always be part of my memories of growing up.

John 'Doddy' Dodimead
Life long City Fan and one time official Bristol City terrace sweeper

I used to go with my dad to all City's games through the seventies. Although the atmosphere could be hostile I think it was the same at most clubs you went to back then, football violence was indicative of those times. As a kid you were aware of it, but because you were amongst your own fans you felt safe and secure inside the ground. Outside was certainly a different kettle of fish, many a time I would take my scarf off and put it in my pocket if we approached opposing fans on the way home or whilst waiting on the bus stop. I started to go to games on my own when I was about 11, this would have been around 1976, which was the start of First Division football for the club and the arrival of footballs top teams. I don't think I can pick any particular game, but I know I watched all of them from behind those red railings of the East End.

It will always be part of my growing up and anybody who does not understand what that part of the ground means to fans or why this book needs to come out has plainly never experienced the highs and lows of following football.

Paul Whittaker
Ex East Ender (Now living in the USA)

One day when I was eight years old, I got ready quickly as I was going to Ashton Gate. The date was 16 February 1974 we were heading off for THAT game, a game that will always stay with me. Leeds United fifth Round FA Cup, a game that everybody thought we had no chance, but not this eight-year-old. Me and my brother Tim who was 10 piled into Dads ford Cortina and of we set for the City. Typically looking back dad got there early as he was worried about somewhere to park (He never changed). We saw some Leeds fans in their colours along with smug condescending grins on their faces as they enjoyed their little trip to the West country on their way too Wembley. As I walked along with my dad and brother I remember peeking out from my snorkel parka and thinking I wonder if City can win the cup? As we entered the East End Tim and me got pushed right to the front against the railings. There were some older City fans behind us so I had that unmistakable aroma of cigarettes, beer and a Wrigley's spearmint gum off them. As the game progressed I remember all the shouts for City and the abuse of the Leeds players but to be honest I never understood some of the songs aimed at these stars of *Match of the Day*. I think we were 1–0 down at half-time but the singing never stopped. My dad who was stood with some of his mates from work came down to us and gave us a packet of crisps and a drink each and told us we will score second half. In the second half Dad was right Keith Fear stuck the ball home and made it 1–1 the East End erupted and I fell on the floor only to be picked up by a group of lads one of which kissed me. When the final whistle blew the ground went crazy, it felt like we had won and too me that day will always be with me. Sadly I lost my dad two years ago and we, along with my brother always used to talk about that day and the joy of the drive home. Dad would love to know that this story is in a book as it was a day that made us SO happy and sometimes those days have been few and far between watching City. I will be sad that the East End has gone but I know the memories never will.

Bob Luton
City Fan

Being a keen City fan I have over the years had many great times in the East End and many heart-breaking moments as well. The East End was always my choice of place to see the City ever since I was 12 years old. After hearing that the old end was too be demolished and City's plans to produce a book of supporters memories I felt compelled to tell a tale of love, fear and above all embarrassment. During the 1975 season I was 14 years old and had become a regular in behind the gap between the goal and the right corner flag. What had drawn me over the season was the arrival of a vision of loveliness dressed in a St John ambulance uniform. She looked a bit older than me but she became the result of me missing quite a few goals that season as I tried to hatch a plan to speak to her. At first I realised that after games the St John ambulance team would congregate in the Winterstoke Road car park behind the East End before going their separate ways, but every time I tried to speak to her she had gone, but I did find out that her name was Sue after hearing one of the brigade call after her as she got in her fathers car to go home. My desperation to meet Sue became so obsessive that I even thought about joining the brigade but then the reality of the piss take I would get from my mates would be too much too bear even if it meant becoming Sue's Boyfriend. I thought of various ways too win her love, one of which included writing notes to her while the game went on then scrunching them up and throwing them at her. But the wind and a bollocking from a copper meant that the gorgeous Sue never got any of them. So with the help of my best mate Dean Cooper we decided that I was to faint during a game I would then be carried out too the waiting Sues arms and 'Bingo' my charm would do the rest. So we started the plan as City played Sheffield Wednesday I collapsed in my usual spot, as the City fans rallied round to help me, my mate Dean got the attention of a policeman stood to the side of the end. He came down and signalled that we needed the St John ambulance. The plan was working perfectly as I looked through squinted eyes waiting for the lovely Sue and one of her colleagues to rescue me. Suddenly two old blokes in St John uniforms and built like prop forwards grabbed me off my feet and proceeded to drag me out of the East End and fought to get me on a stretcher. I recovered remarkably as I fought to stay upright and they fought to put me in a horizontal position and this spectacle suddenly became more interesting than the game and I was aware of people starting to roar with laughter, particularly a pretty colleague of my two wrestling partners. The fight went right in front of the East End and ended when I escaped their clutches and ran out of the ground missing Keith Fears winner. I returned a few games later after all the piss taking from my friends had died down, but sadly I never plucked up the courage too stand near Sue anymore. I would love to end this story by telling you that we lived happily ever after, I saw her at following games but never to talk too and then she disappeared from the St John ambulance. So thanks East End for being the scene of my most embarrassing moment.

Phil Kelly
City Fan still in search of Sue

The East End was like an extra player. It kept the team going, it sucked the ball in, intimidated the opposition, it gave the referee stick. I don't think I could pick out my favourite match or my specific memory. I will always remember night games though. They were better than Saturdays. I think it was because there dark everybody seems that much closer together without realising they are doing it. Sound seems to act in a different way also at night games it reverberates around the ground like at no other time. Especially in the seventies when everybody was smoking and you would catch a glimpse of the smoke on the floodlights. It was magical.

Richard Harptree
City fan exiled in London

I first started going to the East End in the seventies. I loved the atmosphere of the place. There were certainly things that went on there that would not happen anywhere else. I used to regularly grab strangers if we scored or be crushed by some great huge lunatic saying, 'Fucking great mate! I love you!' You had never seen them before but it did not matter.

Jerry Windsor
City Fan

I first went to the City ground during the seventies. I went with my mates from school and we had a great time. In fact I would say that it was my most memorable time supporting City. The East End was 'Our place'. It could be a bit naughty in there, but me and my mates loved the buzz we got from being goaded by the opposition and giving them some banter back. The East End would always start the singing at Ashton Gate and it would travel right round the ground like a fire. We took that same atmosphere to away grounds during the 70s and 80s. When I look back I made so many friends stood in that part of the ground.

Some friends have been with me for years and others have just been friends from 3pm until 4.45. And once the game has ended I wouldn't see them until another home game. After the games we would all have a few drinks in Bedminster, which to be honest was a bit run down at that time. We would then go home and have a sleep on the couch before getting ready for Saturday night at the Naval Volunteer in Kings Street and then The Locarno. Obviously as a fan of the seventies at Ashton Gate I would have to say the promotion night against Portsmouth sticks in my mind. It was a lovely summer evening and I could not believe the atmosphere of the place. The East End was jumping all game and the feeling of running on the pitch at the end is something I will always remember. It was made even sweeter by the fact that I was there with my mates. Another memory is a League Cup game against West Ham in 1975. We drew at Upton Park 0–0 in the first match and got beaten 3–1 in the replay with Paul Cheesley scoring City's goal if I'm right in thinking. West Ham brought thousands down for the game and I remember there being pitch battles in the car park behind the East End after the game as some of the West Ham supporters coaches were parked there. It was really scary but also really exciting for us young lads at the time. I remember throwing rocks and anything I could get hold of at the Hammers fans as they boarded their coaches. Its stupid now when I look back, but I'm afraid that was football on the terraces in the 1970s. It was a dangerous place back then. I still go to City games today and I can't help but notice how well games are policed and how it's all organized. Back in my day we just ran amuck with the police and opposing supporters. The irony of my memory is that I am now a serving Police officer with the Avon and Somerset Constabulary, something that all my mates have found hilarious over the years considering what a nightmare we used to be back then. As a City fan I am excited to see the new stand when its built, but I will always have affection for the old East End.

Simon Leonard
City fan and serving Police officer

Thanks for the opportunity to share my memories of the East End. I think this book is a great idea as I thought it was such a shame that part of the ground is going and there did not seem any type of memorial to it, so peoples memories is, in my opinion really fitting. I first started going to watch Bristol City in the late 1960s with my dad and his mates. The first game I ever saw was a 1–0 win in 1967 against Derby County. Chris Garland got the goal and I was around 13 years of age. Dad and his mates took me into the East End or covered end as they referred to it and I loved it ever since. Don't get me wrong it was nothing to look at and the toilets with no roof on were horrific but the atmosphere the place generated was incredible. I started to go with my mates in the 1970s and we always stood at the back of the East End. I loved it there, we would sing, kick the metal wall at the back and cause as much trouble as possible. I found standing on the East End really exciting in the 1970s, proberbly due to the violence that surrounded the sport in that decade. I made friends for life and it was all down to that part of the ground. God bless you East End you will be sadly missed.

Martin 'Gutter' Gutteridge
City till I die

I remember hearing an advert for this book on Radio Bristol last year. I thought it was a good idea to mark the renovation of that part of the ground and as a City supporter I would certainly buy it. My own memory of the East End is pretty straightforward...fear. In 1975 I got promotion with Midland Bank. I was working in Plymouth and I got a job with the company in Bristol. I was recently married and myself and my wife Alison looked upon this move to 'the big city' as a wonderful opportunity. I was 24 years of age and we moved to a new house in Brislington, Bristol. All my work colleagues liked football and I have to be honest I could take or leave the game. My friends told me that I should support City as I was now from South Bristol. I decided I would go to a game ideally with some work mates but they were busy. So I went on my own and caught the bus from Brislington and got off at Winterstoke Road. I did not really know the geography of the ground so I went straight into the nearest stand which was the East End. I positioned myself at the back by the entranced and waited for the game to kick-off against Portsmouth. The end started to fill up and the atmosphere was incredible although the smell from the toilets still haunt me to this day. City won the game 3–1 but what I will always remember was with about 15 minutes left a gang of what I presume to be Portsmouth fans ran in the East End and there was a massive brawl as City fans and police threw them out. I have never been so scared in all my life and I was shaking all the way home. My workmates laughed their heads off when I told them the next day and they advised me that only the nutjobs go in there. So I never went in the East End ever again. I have supported City for forty years and always from the safety of the Williams stand. My kids and grandkids come with me and they enjoy a good laugh at the story of their hard nut granddad who was pet-rified in the East End.

Stephen Connor
Still in the Williams

I remember having a very wide red and white City scarf that my auntie knitted for me. I used to wear it to games with a City rosette. I got beaten up outside the East End by some Rovers fans after a derby game and they ran off with my scarf and rosette. I must have been about 14 years of age. Looking back I probably deserved it, as I must have looked a right mug. I then progressed to the silk City scarf. I had two and they were tied around my wrists like a proper Eastender. I obviously learnt my lesson.

Paul Thorpe
Exiled City fan living in Doncaster

I loved standing on the East End during the 1970s. When ever I think about those time I always think of Gerry Gow. He optimises the 70s for me. He certainly looked the part with his long hair and moustache and he had no respect for player's reputations, no matter how big a star they were. I have seen Gerry Dominate some of the 1970s finest players. And lets not forget Gerry could play a bit too. My mates and me used to love shouting him on as he got stuck into an opposing midfielder from the East End. I remember one game about 1978 we drew 2–2 with Everton Gerry had already made his mark when he had Everton's Andy King by the throat for a off the ball elbow. We all started singing 'Oh Gerry, Gerry. Gerry, Gerry, Gerry, Gerry, Gerry Gow' and minutes later he scored and blew the East End a kiss. He was a real top player who gave 100% and City fans through the years only ever ask for 100%. I met him years later when he was landlord of the White Horse in West Street and I was not disappointed to meet a hero, he really was something special. So when they tear down the East End I will think of the days watching Gerry Gow from those Terraces.

Alan Peacock
City Fan

I am pleased that I can get the opportunity to send you my memories of standing in the East End. I first started going to the City ground when I was a kid with my dad. This would have been the 1960s and we used to stand in front of the Williams stand but as I got older I was drawn like many of my mates towards the East End. It was a tough old place back then but when we got to about 13 or 14 me and mates started going to games on our own and it was the East End for us. The one memory I will have of the East End would be the FA Cup tie against Leeds United in 1973–74 season. I was 14 and for one thing I could not believe we were playing the mighty Leeds United with all those internationals. We beat Hereford in the fourth round away and I had gone with my mate Peter Tomkins and his dad. I think Geoff Merrick got the goal and on the way back all we could do was talk about who we wanted in the next round. The draw was made on Monday lunchtime and all the City fans at school crowded round a small transistor radio we had brought in. When it was Leeds at home we all screamed and even some of the teachers told us they could not believe the draw. So when that February day arrived I could not wait to get to the game. Tome and me caught the bus from Headley Park where we lived and got to Ashton Gate about 12.30pm that gave us enough time to see Leeds arrive on their coach. We got a glimpse of a few stars but we had no chance of an autograph, as it was about five deep around the player's entrance. Although we did get the chance to sing, 'City, City, City'. We then got into the East End and it was already filling up. We were so excited that by the time kick-off arrived we were set explode. I have never ever experienced an atmosphere like it. These were the days when the FA Cup was a massive incentive to big clubs so there was none of this resting top players. All Leeds United's top players were there and playing against our Bristol City. I will always remember

Keith Fears goal, I think the roof nearly came off the East End. I don't remember who scored for Leeds but we were happy with a replay. We were buzzing on the way home, but we could not get to the replay as it was mid-week and in the afternoon. This was so Leeds did not have to use the floodlights in the middle of the energy crisis. Still a packed Elland Road saw us win 1–0 through a Donnie Gillies goal. It was a massive cup shock at the time and we drew the eventual winners Liverpool in the next round. Again the East End was buzzing as we unfortunately lost 1–0. But I will always remember that cold afternoon stood on the East End when Leeds came to town. Looking back I think it was the first time I had seen the players from *Match of The Day* in the flesh.

Gerry Ford
Bristol City fan for life

PAUL CHEESLEY

To the fans who stood on the terraces during the 1970s they had one hero and that was Paul Cheesley. From the banner that proclaimed during the famous Portsmouth promotion night 'Cheeseley walks on cider' to the reception this popular ex-player gets by the fans when he attends games at Ashton Gate today, their love of this talented centre-forward will never be forgotten. Paul was born in Bristol but rejected by both Bristol clubs as a youngster and it was at Norwich City that he would gain first team football under the guidance of boss Ron Saunders. But City realising what they had missed had a £30,000 bid accepted by new Norwich Manager John Bond and another piece of the young talented team Alan Dicks was putting together at Ashton Gate was secured. Paul possessed a thunderous shot in either foot and this mixed with speed, great timing and bravery made for a potent striker. In 1975 England manager at the time Don Revie called Paul into the England under-23 squad but as this was City's promotion season he chose to play for the Robins in a league match but their seemed little doubt that he would get his call again. With City gaining promotion on a hot night at Ashton Gate, Paul would explode onto the football stage getting the only goal in City's opening game in the top flight as they beat Arsenal at Higbury. Then three days after the glory of Highbury Paul twisted his knee in City's home game against Stoke City after a collision with Stoke 'keeper Peter Shilton. Months of operations followed but Paul was lost to League football forever. What Paul Cheesley could of done in the game will forever be a talking point, but for East End fans he did enough for them to love him forever.

I used to go to Ashton Gate when I was a kid. Sometimes with my uncle or with my mates. We would get the bus from Easton-in-Gordano and it would cost sixpence for a return. We always stood in the East End or covered end as it was then. I remember watching great players like Gordon Low, Jantzen Derrick, Jack Connor and Mike Gibson, I never thought that one day there would be people in the East End shouting my name. Ashton Gate had a real buzz to it then there were buses all around the ground ferrying people to the match and I remember Ashton Road which lead to the railway bridge being absolutely jammed with peoples bikes, in fact most gardens were packed as fans parked their bikes and residents charged

them. Obviously I have a lot of affection for the City fans par-
ticularly the ones who used to stand in the East End. I have a
photo at home with a picture of the crowd on the promotion
night against Portsmouth and they have a banner that said
'Cheesly walks on cider'. They spelt my name wrong but I will
forgive them that. The feeling I got that night when I saw that
banner will remain with me forever. They always created a
massive atmosphere around the ground when the East End
started to get going, you could really feel it on the pitch. That's
why I was so upset when they put away fans in part of the
end as due to the acoustics of the stand they seemed to make
more noise than the home fans who were in the Atyeo stand. I
remember when I got my injury I went for a ball in the air with
Peter Shilton and I fell awkwardly and I knew right away it
was serious. I had never known pain like it as I had appar-
ently ripped my cartilage, tore ligaments and chipped a bone
in my knee. I did it at the open end of the ground but I could
still hear the East End fans singing my name, which was won-
derful. I will be sad to see the end go but I love the idea of the
new stand and I hope it gets filled every other week with City
fans who make some noise for the team.

PAUL CHEESLEY
BRISTOL CITY: 1973–77
APPEARANCES: 73
GOALS: 21

My favourite memory from standing in the East End has to
be the game against Liverpool in 1977. I was about 14 years
old and Liverpool had won the league and were preparing

for the Cup Final on the following Saturday. The East End was rammed to capacity and I was hanging off a girder at the back of the end. I'm told there were nearly 40,000 in Ashton Gate for that game and I am not surprised. I was with all my mates in the rafters of the stands and the noise was incredible it sounded like a jet engine. The wonderful Chris Garland got the goals as we beat them 2–1 although I never saw any of the goals go in. It was a magical game and we walked back to Stockwood where I lived as we could not get on a bus as there was no room. We had a great time when we went back to school. I think I made it my personal mission to find every Liverpool fan in the school and give them stick …Happy Days.

Ray 'Fudger' Wilks
Eastender through the 70s and 80s

I don't have any particular game that I remember from the seventies, to be honest there were loads of matches that I could have thought of but if I'm honest my memories of the East End are of the songs we sung they still make me laugh today as they were really of their time and not very PC in todays world.

I was born under an East End star
I was born under an East End star
Knives are made for stabbing
Guns are made to shoot
If you meet the East End
You're sure to get the boot

I'd like to buy a ball and chain and fill it with lead
And when I saw a Rovers fan id wrap it round his head
AG, AGR, AGRO, AGRO
AG, AGR, AGRO, AGRO

*If you go down to the woods today, you're sure of a big
surprise*
*If you go down to the woods today you will never believe
your eyes*
*Cos Jeremy bear the sugar puff bear has bought some
boots and cropped his hair*
And gone to join the East End boot boys

We hate Nottingham Forest
We hate Liverpool too
We hate Bristol Rovers
But City we love you

We had joy we had fun
We had Rovers on the run
But the joy did not last
Cos the bastards ran too fast
Hello, Hello City Agro, City Agro Hello
I'm a bow legged chicken
I'm a knock-kneed hen
I aint been so happy since I don't know when
I walk with a wiggle and a wiggle and a walk
Doing the East End boot walk.

Loved all these songs hope you can put them in the book.

Peter Webb
City fan

I remember getting wacked across the head by a coppers truncheon whilst trying to get out of the East End and onto the pitch after the Portsmouth game. It never hurt until I got home then a massive lump appeared on the back of my head. It was worth it though that was a great night for every City fan. I certainly won't forget it even though I probably should have gone for a check up at the hospital.

Tim Evans

GEOFF MERRICK

To Many supporters Geoff Merrick will always be remembered as one of the Ashton Eight, a group of players who ripped up their contracts in the 1980s to help secure the future of the club. But we should never forget the incredible contribution this local talented footballer gave to Bristol City from the moment he made his debut in 1968 to that dreadful day when he and the other seven players were put in an inexcusable position by the club. Geoff was an England schoolboy international who was only ever going to play for his local club even though the likes of Liverpool and Aston Villa had expressed an interest. A quick centre-back with a ferocious tackle he had that rare ability of being able to read the game like no other. He progressed to captain of the club by the time he was 20 years of age. Merrick lead

Bristol City towards the ultimate prize of top-level football in the 1975–76 season. An inquiry from Arsenal fell on deaf ears, as Merrick stayed loyal to the club. Even the arrival of Norman Hunter and a switch to left back could not shake Merricks consistency at the back for City. Geoff was a man who had been at the very heart of the good times with City and in 1981–82 season he would find himself at the very heart of the darkest days for the club. Merrick and seven colleagues Gerry Sweeney, Chris Garland, David Rogers, Peter Aitken, Trevor Tainton, Jimmy Mann and Julian Marshall were told of the clubs financial plight and for City to survive they would have to rip up their contracts in order for the club, as they were the top earners. The players were put under tremendous pressure by the club and media, so rip up the contracts they did. Geoff left the club and headed along with Chris Garland for a stint in Hong Kong but returned months later. Spells in the non-league scene followed with Bath City, Yeovil and Bridgewater Town before Geoff hung up his boots in his mid forties. Today he runs a successful building company in Bristol. Geoff Merrick was truly a local lad who loved the club and his actions in 1981 proved that.

I will always have great affection for the City fans and especially the East End lads. As I ran out I would always have a look up at the East End. They always gave the side a great reception and my God did they make some noise. I first went to City with my dad and we stood on the East End with him. We would walk from our house on the Chessels. We lived in Garnett Street and all the lads around were City fans. I used to dream about playing for the club one day. Dad like many before him would put me on the fencing then go and stand with the men at the back of the end. Every father seemed to do it and down the front it was full of kids and you never felt threatened in the slightest as you knew your dad was behind you.

When I was captain in the 1970s the East End was a wall of sound for the players, it was always the place where the chanting started and the singing got louder and louder. As a player you are always aware of the noise the crowd makes and it can give you goose bumps when you are playing. But I do have a memory for the book and that is whilst I was playing I would have one voice that I got to know very well but I never met the gentleman and I would love to even now. You see he would shout 'Your shit Merrick' or 'Get off Merrick you wanker'. When I would turn round all I would see was a crowd of people and I would never see the culprit. I am not that conceited to think that I never had a bad game and when I did I would take it on the chin, but this would be happening whatever the score even if we were 3–0 up I would still get 'Merrick you tosser'. So I hope he writes in and tells us that his memory of the East End is abusing Geoff Merrick through the 1970s maybe we can have a pint. I will miss the East End as it was such a symbol of some great times the club had. I hope the new stand will bring some good times for the future.

GEOFF MERRICK
BRISTOL CITY: 1967–81
APPEARANCES: 427
GOALS: 13

RAY CASHLEY

Ray Cashley was truly a man who had big boots to fill. Ray had the unenviable task of taking over from the popular Mike Gibson in the City goal. Ray made his debit for City in an FA Cup tie against Southampton and never looked back. Cashley certainly had an unconventional route to the top, joining City as a youngster as a full-back. But when the Bristol City youth team were struggling for a 'keeper it was the young Cashley who got the chance of the green shirt that became his own. Cashley was certainly not your archetypal 'keeper standing around 5ft 9in but what he lacked in height he more then made up for in bravery and shot stopping. Although he was certainly not the finished article Ray would spend hours on the Bristol City training pitch working with the coaching staff in order to make him a better player. Cashley would become a firm favourite with the fans although sometimes he would have them covering their eyes as he came storming off his line trying to retrieve a ball he would never get. But City fans realised this local lad gave everything for the club and that's all supporters ask for. Mention the name Ray Cashley today and somebody will certainly recall the night of the 18 September 1973. City were at home to Hull City and it was a wet and windy affair City had gone 1–0 down and then striker Tom Ritchie pulled one back to make it 1–1. Ray with his back to the East End bounced the ball then let fly with an awesome goal-kick that seemed to stay in the air forever. The ball bounced on Hull's 18 yard box and flew over the tigers 'keeper Jeff Whealands and straight into the Hull net to make it 2–1. City went on to win the game 3–1 but the following day every schoolboy in every playground in south Bristol was trying to do a Ray Cashley and score from a goal-kick. As City found themselves in the top flight Ray would find his form dipping in and out and suddenly he fell behind number two 'keepers John Shaw who was a recent signing from Leeds United. He left the club in 1980–81 season and signed for rivals Bristol Rovers where he made 50 appearances, after that he ended his career at Chester City. Ray will always be fondly remembered by the fans if only for that wet night in September.

I am really pleased to be asked to contribute to this wonderful book. I have a great admiration for the fans at the East End. I loved my time at City and the fans were great to me but there was something about the fans at that end. I don't know whether it was the way the stand was built but it seemed to be a cauldron of noise that used to send shivers up my spine when they got going. I loved those fans because they gave me time to settle in. They loved Mike Gibson but I will be forever indebted to them for giving me a chance. When they cheered my name I felt 10 feet tall. I also want to say that I could hear every little remark they would make and there were some funny guys in that end. Everybody asks me about the Hull City game and that match along with the Portsmouth night has to be up there with my favourites. The Hull game was a wet and windy night and I loved playing under the floodlights, as there was something magical about night games. We were 1–0 down then Tom Ritchie got one back for us. I had a goal-kick and I just put my foot right through it as I always did. I remember seeing it in the night sky and I saw the back of the net move down the open end but to be honest I thought it had bounced of the wall at the end and hit the netting. Suddenly the whole ground went silent. I don't think anybody knew what to do.

Apparently Keith Fear ran up to the ref and said, 'That's a goal, that's a goal' and the ref agreed and blew his whistle. The East End behind me went mental. I remember every time I got the ball the fans in the East End were shouting, 'shoot, shoot, shoot'. It was a bizarre night that I will never forget. I am told that Pat Jennings did it and Peter Shilton and I was the third. I look at the types of balls today and the boots and I think I could of done it every week in today's football.

RAY CASHLEY
BRISTOL CITY: 1970–71, 1980–81
APPEARANCES: 261
GOALS: 1

My favourite era watching City was the 1970s and I spent that like all my friends in the East End. They were special times. Saturdays match would be in our thoughts all week. When I left work on a Friday we couldn't wait for the Saturday morning. We would go and have a Breakfast in a café in West Street. Im sure it was called something like Deordas. Me and my mates would then go and have bet in a Betting office up by the Hen and Chicken and usually see City midfielder Gerry Gow knocking about in there. We always shouted, 'Hey Gerry we won't tell Dicksy'. Then it was a pub-crawl until about 2.40pm when we would squeeze our way into the East End for the match. The noise that place created was immense we would sing our hearts out. And after it would be another few pints before wash and change and off up to the Towns Talk club, Platform One or The Webbington where we would see some of the players

again. They were great days before I got married a.
responsibilities and the East End was part of those days. ₁
will miss her

Len Watkins
Birmingham

Throughout the seventies City had a fearsome reputation
in the Second Division around the East End. All the lads
had the David Bowie look of Ziggy Stardust and there had
been some massive altercations with our friends across
the water Cardiff City along with Leeds United in the FA
Cup and Spurs. The East End grew in popularity amongst
some of the young supporters as the place to be. And when
the club gained promotion in 1976 things got more turbu-
lent on the terraces with the likes of Arsenal, Manchester
United and Villa visiting Ashton Gate and wanting to test
the mettle of the East End. I have to say we never let the
visiting fans down.

Tom Hopegood
City fan

I was 21 in 1976, a seasoned campaigner down Ashton
Gate and the Guildhall Tavern, an underground soul-funk
venue in the centre of Bristol, featuring DJs such as the
Ashby Brothers, Steve and Adrian. Now 40 years on I am
fighting a losing battle with Parkinson's, in its fifth year but
there are people a lot worse of than me.

It was a roasting hot September in 1976, as I walked

along Coronation Road in my 'Peg' trousers, pointed shoes from Clobber, situated by the bus station and a red and black striped bowling shirt. This was the 'de rigueur' uniform of the Avon soul army. I reached the metal bridge by the Albion pub and saw spider woman, a girl I knew from The Guildhall and entered into some small talk. When out of the corner of my eye, I noticed 15 to 20 grown men snaking their way across the bridge in single file, trying to look part of the scenery, but no chance, to my trained eye, these were West Ham. Making my excuses, I walked further down the road to the 'Try Again' pub, hoping to find some City boys, but no. The place was empty, so I quickly moved down to the Gate to spread the word. After a few pints I made my way into the 'East End', the covered terrace where we stood to sing and chant our team onto victory and the end we defended against rival fans.

The first one I noticed coming in was a tall black man in a pin-striped suit, a Mungo Jerry Afro and side burns. He took up a position just where the East End roof started on the corner of the terrace. This man was Cass Pennant a member of the West Ham firm run by Ted Buigsby and Bunter Marks, the Teddy Bunter firm or 'TBF'. Then another came in, faded blue denim bib and brace, Ox blood loafers with ice blue tassels (West Ham colours) and he had 'Henna' on his hair. I saw my first punk that day, he had metal shin guards on his boots from Malcolm McLaren's shop 'BOY' on the Kings Road in London and a red beret. *I'm forever blowing bubbles* started to rise above the cacophony of sound, a battle cry, were on your manor, do what you will.

'Crash' two armies clashed together blood splattered over red berets and loafers. 'United United' went the battle anthem as two groups swayed to and fro, trying to gain the upper hand. Crunch went the truncheons on heads and order was restored. West Ham was ushered out across the pitch to a standing ovation from their compatriots in the open end.

Its ironic now almost 45 years on, I am friends with a few Hammers including Mr Pennent, Some of those who were there that day are no longer with us, but memories like these were part of the East End folklore. 'And you know what, I wouldn't change a thing'.

Roger Trainer
Life long City fan, Keynsham

5.

THE EIGHTIES

After the grim filled decade that was the 1970s, the 80s will always be remembered as a decade of excess and 'loadsamoney'. It was a time when Britain's first female Prime Minister Margret Thatcher rolled out her vision for Britain. It was a vision that would have council tenants given the opportunity to buy their council houses, Ordinary workers would become shareholders in companies and she promoted a manifesto that encouraged people to start businesses and get on. Thatcher also decided that she would deal with the country's unions or, 'The enemy within' as she described them. There would be no more union bosses calling into number ten to tell the Government what to do, which had happened when Labour were in power and she was certainly not going to be held to ransom by them as previous Conservative Prime Ministers had done. Instead she decided to take them on and although she would be the eventual winner in this heavyweight encounter, it was at a dreadful cost to communities through out the country as coal pits and steel works closed making millions unemployed. She created a flag waving culture within the middle classes of the UK and this was never more prevalent than when she sent British troops to the Falkland Isles after the Argentinian invasion. The troops returned triumphant and the decision to send them gave way for her to see another four years in office. Thatcher certainly polarised the country as for every flag waving middle class there was a section of the population that grew more and more resentful and disenfranchised with society, and that was mainly the young. Early in her term of office there were riots in Brixton London, Handsworth Birmingham, Toxteth Liverpool and the St Pauls area of Bristol as the young black population grew more and more angry at the predominantly white police forces' policy on stop and search, a policy that was widely pushed by the Conservative government at the time. Although Thatcher's Britain promoted prosperity the truth was that there were areas of the country that were in desperate need of rejuvenation. A perfect example of this was the south of Bristol and in particularly the Ashton and Bedminster areas that saw shops closing along with factories after the departure of WH Wills in the 70s and the consequenting move of the workforce to the Hartcliffe area of Bristol.

For football fans this was an era when they were universally hated. The violence that had blighted the 1970s terraces was becoming more and more sophisticated as rival 'Firms' formed and travelled to more away games looking for trouble than their 1970s predecessors. The fashion amongst the terraces had also taken on a new look as bovver boots and skinheads became replaced with wedge haircuts and designer sportswear such as Nike, Fila, Sergio Tachinni and Lacoste along with the Stanley knife that had now become the weapon of choice. The introduction of designer wear is rumoured to have been brought in by Liverpool fans who were always in Europe watching their club and decided to bring back some of the fashions. At first the look certainly made it more difficult to spot troublemakers for the police as the wearing of any club colours was now defunked. But as the decade grew it became the terrace look. As with the preceeding decades music was still very important on the terraces with bands such as The Jam and The Specials becoming favourites. This would also be mixed with a love of Soul and Funk music. As the police started to tighten up on home grown violence the 1980s would see more and more fans follow the national team away and this gained momentum in 1982 when England played in the World Cup in Spain. It was a massive thing for the hooligans as England had not been to a world cup since 1970 in Mexico. For the majority of football fans their reputation sank further and further into the mire as scenes of violence were constantly splashed across TV and newspapers. These incidents would be justification enough for many who wanted football fans closely monitored and this also brought about the Thatcher governments push to bring in an ID membership scheme for all fans. Thatcher wanted the scheme to spread nationwide. It offered power over fans; legislation for it was included in the football spectator's act, restricting access to grounds to anyone who had not signed up for the scheme. Anyone who was not a member would be liable on summary of conviction to imprisonment of up to one month. The treatment of supporters only added to the conflict towards the police of even the most law-abiding citizens. Football fans indiscriminately were treated like cattle and herded into pens at grounds up and down the country. The early 1980s would see crowds falling. The game was seldom on TV and there was even a time when ITN stopped giving out the football results. The game was going downhill fast. It took a number of tragedies to stop fans in their tracks. One was a summer's night in the Heysel Stadium,

Belgium and another was a summer's afternoon in Sheffield. The Heysel disaster saw fans fleeing the fighting between Liverpool and Juventus fans at the 1985 European Cup Final. It resulted in a wall collapsing with 39 fatalities and 600 injured. The incident was described as UEFA darkest hour. The incident would see British clubs banned from European Football until the 1990s. At home there was the Hillsborough tragedy where 96 Liverpool fans lost their life at the FA Cup semi-final against Nottingham Forest at Hillsborough, Sheffield Wednesdays ground. Combined with the Bradford fire disaster where 56 fans lost their lives when the main stand caught fire at Bradford's Valley Parade ground whilst Bradford played Lincoln City in 1985. This particular disaster would change how authorities would build future grounds. So great was the hatred of football fans at the time that it took over 25 years before the fans at Hillsborough were exonerated and the disaster was found to be the result of negligence on behalf of the police. But to some mud sticks even to this day. After the Hillsborough tragedy Lord Justice Taylor was invited to look at the way football was run and what changes could be made to ensure the safety of its supporters. The first thing he did was to throw out the ID membership scheme. The act was full of ill-informed arrogance towards supporters from a government who had no real understanding of the average football supporter. Lord Justice Taylor himself called the idea 'like using a sledge hammer to crack a walnut'. Lord Justice Taylor identified the need for change as in the lead up to Hillsborough stadiums were primitive affairs with fencing. Men would urinate against walls or into sinks at half-time due to lack of facilities. And any women who went to games would struggle to find a toilet in some grounds. The Taylor report would become one of the most fundamental changes the game would ever see. The report would conclude amongst other things that standing up at football games was fundamentally dangerous. And the recommendation was that all Premier League and First Division grounds, at least must be all seater by 1994.

Off the pitch Ashton Gate would find itself playing host to everything from The Rolling Stones to an international cricket match involving the rest of the world v England. The club also put a new roof on the East End and called it The Wedlock stand after their legendary England player of the 1900s Billy 'Fatty' Wedlock. Shirt advertising was also introduced as the club sported local car hire company Hirerite across their shirts. On the pitch the 1980s would test the resolve of even the most passionate City fan. The club were relegated back to Division Two in 1980–81 and Alan Dicks was dismissed. The financial position of the club was also disclosed in 1981. It appeared that they were in debt to the tune of £700,000 and by 1982 the club looked to be on the brink of closing. In fact many supporters thought the away game of 30 January against Newport County in 1982 would be the clubs last. Supporters rallied round to raise cash and Directors fought long and hard to try and find a solution. The plan they came up with was to start a new organisation known as Bristol City 1982. The plan worked in principle but it depended on the acceptance of the top wage earners and players with the longest contracts accepting a redundancy package. The players involved were known as the Ashton Eight. The country's media became camped outside a Bristol hotel, as this solution had never been asked of a group of players in modern football. As club directors along with the eight and their PFA representatives tried to strike a deal in the hotel room. Then on

2 February 1982 an hour before the deadline ended, the players agreed and emerged from the room. They agreed to rip up their contracts to save the club and accept the redundancy package. This cleared the way for a new organisation to take charge of the club. Geoff Merrick, Jimmy Mann, Peter Aitken, Julian Marshall, David Rodgers, Chris Garland, Trevor Tainton and Gerry Sweeney shared £82,000 and will always be remembered by supporters, as would Directors like Ken Sage and Deryn Collier who also fought to save the club. It was a very dark day in the history of the club. The pain would still not ease as by 1983–84 season City found themselves in Division Four. Managers such as Bob Houghton and Roy Hodgson (Yes the now England manager) could not stop the fall from grace. But the appointment of Terry Cooper breathed some life into the club by promoting youngsters from within, such as former schoolboys Rob Newman and Andy Llewellyn who found themselves playing first team football when barely out of their teens. Coopers philosophy was born mainly out of necessity but his shrewd work in the transfer market meant that maybe the club could get back to former glories. Cooper would guide the club to two Wembley appearances in the Freight Rover Trophy and a promotion before leaving his post in 1988. Former player Joe Jordan took the rains and took City to within a whisker of Division Two by the end of the decade. It had been a tortuous decade for the club but there were glimmers of light on the horizon, as surely the next decade could not get any worse?

As a teenager in the late 80s my one vivid memory was in a packed East End watching Sheffield United in the play-offs wearing white stiletto shoes!!!! What was I thinking!!!!

Sarah
(Now 40 something sitting in the Williams stand)

Always remember watching City in the East End and a bloke behind me giving City full-back Andy Llewellyn advice all game on being aware of their winger 'Llewellyn wing, wing, wing' he kept shouting until some bloke at the back of the East End screamed, 'Someone answer that Fucking Phone'. The whole section where I was fell about laughing. thats what I loved about the East End, the humour.

Jim Stevens
East Ender until the away fans went in

Hereford in the Freight Rover semi-final second leg. We were 2–0 down from the first leg and all hope seemed to have gone but we were terrific that night. We were winning 2–0 on the night, so 2–2 on aggregate when the game went to extra-time. I was dying to go to the toilet but held it in and held it in until I could hold on no longer. As I made my way through the fans in the East End to the toilets Alan Walsh crossed for Steve Neville to score and send us to Wembley for the first time. The place erupted and I fell to the floor and was trampled all over by City fans whilst I was on the floor my bowels decided to fill my trousers there and then. It was a long embarrassing walk home but a wonderful night.

Pete Deaton
Always goes before kick-off

My first experience of football was in the East End, somewhere around 1984–85, in the days of the terraces and railings. Being only about four at the time you can imagine how hard it would be for a small person to see the action, so my grampy made a little wooden seat that used to fix over the railings. During games I used to sit attached to the wall holding onto the railings, with my legs dangling through the gap in the bars, whilst developing admiration for Howard Pritchard! I do apologise now for anybody's view I blocked. I did fall out of love with football shortly after, but returned in the mid nineties and made the Ateyo my home, but I will always have memories of that wooden seat in the East End.

Chris Warner

I loved going to see City in the eighties, got a real buzz from the place, it was my favourite era. I started going as a little kid in the seventies but when I got to my teens the East End was always the place to be. I remember seeing a bloke there called Cyprus Bob and me my mates used to buy knocked off Lacoste, Kappa and Sergio Tachini polo tops off him and if City won it was a bonus.

Tony Earlstone
City fan and Snappy dresser in the 1980s

The end of the 1980s was when I started to fall out of love for the East End. The club had taken the ridiculous decision to move away supporters into part of the end and that really was as far as I am concerned the beginning of the end of this great structure. Football was changing and although I was not happy with seats being installed it was something the club had to do after the recent football tragedies at Hillsborough and Heysel. The whole football violence thing has grown in force, but we all started to move out and go in the Dolman stand or the Williams stand. I will be sad to see the end go, as it created a wonderful atmosphere and it was a great meeting place for me and my mates. I will also miss the old click of the turnstiles but I suppose football has to move on.

Angus
City Terrace Legend

There are many games that I watched in the East End following City, but the one that stands out is the game a week before my 15th birthday. It is the Southern Area semi-final of the Freight Rover Trophy. Having lost the first leg at Hereford United 0–2 City struggled to make the break though in the first-half with very few chances. City knew that they had to score in the second-half and the game changed just after an hour when City scored twice inside a minute, as Riley's header went in the net of the East End followed by a deflected shot that sent the City fans wild. Hereford came close in normal time hitting the bar and coming close in extra-time with a great save by City 'keeper Waugh. But just as we thought it was going to penalties Neville popped up and calmly put a shot into the bottom corner to send my home town club to Wembley. City had made history by getting to Wembley for the first time in their history.

Kevin Brake

The 1980s were in my opinion the very last swansong of the East End. The young lads that had continued to go in the end through the seventies now found themselves as the older leaders amongst the fans. Football violence had changed, as had the fans that got involved. Gone were the bovver boots, scarves and skinhead haircuts. We were now talking the casual look, which consisted of expensive trainers, Designer clothes and no scarves or any team colours, and the violence had a more organised feel to it with fans contacting rival fans in advance. The casual look was brought to the terraces by Liverpool fans who had toured Europe with their club and picked up clothes by Lacoste, Fila, Adidas and Sergio Tachini and all these things found there way to the East End in the 1980s. There was also a large groundswell of City fans who went away with England, which was certainly not the case during the 1970s. This was partly due to us getting fed up of the number of Scottish fans who invaded Wembley every other year. So with the World Cup in Spain in 1982 England fans decided they would descend on the place and have continued to support England in every corner of the globe. I always get a kick out of seeing a banner somewhere in the world where

England are playing that says something like BRISTOL CITY EAST END. Events through the 1980s resulted in me loosing a bit of love for our game and particularly the naughty stuff I was getting up too. The Heysel Stadium disaster, Bradford Fire, and of course Hillsborough. We loved having a laugh but people should never loose their lives watching football and the government and in particular Margret Thatcher came after people like me and football fans in general branding all of them hooligans. Clubs had no choice on the recommendation of the Taylor report to install seats in standing areas and that led to the end really of the East End. I know there will be a whole generation of new fans who won't remember the end for what is was as they remember it for having seats and away fans in. You only have to ask people of a certain age about the East End and they will say, 'It was never the same when they put the seats in'. I will miss it as I had some fantastic times in it but as a City fan I realise the club have too move on and create its own memories for the next generation, I just don't think they will be as 'naughty' as ours.

John Doddy Dodimead
City Fan

First time I ever went to the East End I must have been 14 years old. Some of my mates were regulars on the East End. One particular guy, Martin Shonnell who was two years older than me, used to go everywhere with City and we became friends during the summer, so I went with him for the first match of the 1982–83 season against Hull

City a game we won 2–1. We walked into the East End and although this was a Division Four game the noise that was generated grabbed me and I was hooked. Martin seemed to know everybody so as I was with him everybody accepted me. Martin and his mates stood at the back of the stand and proceeded to start the chants. I never really knew the words but I understood Bristol Rovers Shit, Shit, Shit. My family were the epitome of middle class Britain and they had no interest in football, but I loved shouting singing and in all honestly acting like a twat for an afternoon. I really got caught up in the whole excitement of the atmosphere and suddenly for no apparent reason I grabbed a discarded apple that lay at my feet and launched it towards the front of the end near the railings.

I really did feel like one of the lads as Martin and his mates laughed and jeered. After about 10 minutes I became aware of a massive bloke comforting a small child whilst chatting to a group of City fans. They were pointing in my direction and I felt all the blood drain from my body as this mountain of a bloke started to walk up the steps of the East End towards me, getting bigger and bigger as he got nearer. Suddenly I felt very alone as Martin and his mates seemed to have disappeared around me. 'Did you chuck that fucking apple?' he shouted at me. My mouth became very dry and I felt myself getting redder and redder as I said meekly 'Yes sorry'. 'You hit my daughter you twat' he replied and then proceeded to grab me round the neck and told me that I was very lucky he did not get the apple and push it up my arse, I agreed immediately that I was very lucky. With that he turned and went back to his kids.

Within minutes Martin and his mates re-appeared and told me that they would have smashed his head in, had they in truth not gone and hid. I continued to go and stand in the East End and was always wary of seeing my mate with the kids, but I will never forget my first time in the East End.

James Wilton
One Luck City Fan

I started going in the East End in the early 1980s. It was still the heart of Ashton Gate in my opinion, the place where all the noise was generated. It had a bit of notoriety from the 1970s as a place where all the hard nuts went but I just loved it for the atmosphere in there. You knew there were City fans who were up to no good but that was just part and parcel of football in the eighties. When I look back it was a era when you saw fans starting to wear replica kits, in the seventies you never saw anybody stood on the terraces with replica tops. Me and my mates all had the home shirt with HIRERITE on. In fact I still have it, but I know it wont fit me now that's for sure. You could tell we didn't want any trouble as we did not have Lacoste or Kappa clothes on. I have loads of memories of different games but my most memorable would have too been the 1982–83 season. As a club we were on our arse in the fourth Division under Terry Cooper as we entertained Wimbledon who were flying high at the top of the league. But we beat them 4–2 and Glyn Riley got a hat-trick as we all went mental. There were quite a few young local lads in the side due to us not having any money but they played their heart out and as fans we never forgot that. I don't know why but I will always remember the Wimbledon game, I suppose its because nobody gave us a chance.

Peter Woods
Lifelong City fan

I have been supporting Bristol City for over 60 years, so as you can imagine I have known good times and some terrible times at the club. I first went to Ashton Gate in the 1954–55 season with my uncle. I remember being really excited as we left my Lawrence Weston house. The game was against Norwich City and City lost 1–0 but it did not put me off as I was hooked. As I said I have seen all the ups and downs and I have had the privilege of seeing some great players at the Gate. I have also seen some great players in the red shirt of the Robins. People like Tommy Burdon, Alex Tate and my very favourite John Atyeo. When I first went to Ashton Gate I watched games in the number one stand which is now the Dolman. Then I progressed to the open end and ended up in the Williams stand where I have stayed. I have never watched a City game from the East End, but I did watch a cricket game from there. It was England verses the rest of the world. I remember the game being advertised in the 1980s and I thought it would be fun to see. The England team had some great players in the side like Ian Botham, Mike Gatting, Graham Gooch and Geoff Boycott. It was really odd to not only see cricket on the Ashton Gate pitch but to see it from a side of the ground I had never been to even though I had been going to the ground for years. I remember Geoff Boycott was fielding just in front of the East End and he did not have a lot to do as most of the rest of the world team were scoring runs in one and two batches. Geoff ended up getting a lot of stick from us, but he took it in good part and even signed autographs for fans as the game was going on. I remember there were about 8,000 fans in the ground and the rest of the world won, probably because Geoff Boycott was too busy entertaining us in the East End.

Ben Biggs
City fan for over 60 years

I first heard about the idea for this book whilst driving to my home in Bath on a Friday night. BBC Radio Bristol were talking about fans memories for the East End at Ashton Gate. The conversation brought back a wonderful memory I have of being at that part of the ground. I am no football fan and I could count on one hand the number of times I have set foot in Ashton Gate. My great love is music and I used to spend my late teens following the local music scene watching bands like The X certs, Blue Aeroplanes, Vice Squad and The Various Artists. I got to know many of the bands and one in particular was the reggae band Talisman. They were six lads from St Pauls and they had a bit of local success. I knew a guy called Brendan and he managed the band. They were playing the Trinity Road Church one Saturday night and the place was packed. Brendan came over to me and told me that they had got a spot supporting The Rolling Stones at Ashton

Gate on their European tour. I could not believe it, as this was a real step up for the band. The gig was about a month away and I could not wait for it. Then the day arrived 27 June 1982. Brendan called me the night before and asked if I would like to come to the sound check. I couldn't believe it. He told me he would meet me at the East End part of the ground as that's where they would be bringing their gear in from as the Stones had all the room at the other end where the stage was. I arrived about 1pm and met Brendan and the rest of the band who were so excited it was incredible. Talisman played two songs then finished their sound check. Brendan told me to stay on as the stones were scheduled to go through some of their set but apparently it all depended on Jagger. They had had a late night at the Grand Hotel the night before where they were staying. It seems he wanted to stay there as in the 1960s while they were playing the Colston Hall he was thrown out of the Grand for wearing jeans in the restaurant. Myself and some of the band along with their friends and families sat right at the end of the East End as it had started to rain. We waited for the Stones then about 4pm they walked onto the stage and played *Under my thumb*, *Brown Sugar*, *Honky Tonk Woman* then Jagger left and Keith Richard played a few solos on his own. The experience was magical. To be sat in the football ground with what seemed your own personal gig was a memory that I will never forget. The main gig was fantastic and I was pleased for the Talisman lads as they got a great reception. The Stones were awesome even with the rain. After I managed to get Ronnie Woods autograph, which I still have. So that's my memory of the East End. I hope it will be ok as its not City related but I had one of the greatest afternoons of my life sat on that cold terrace. As for the Talisman lads well they never made it big but are still touring around. As for the Stones well they are doing ok also.

Terry Pritchard
Bath

I loved going in the East End in the 1980s. It was a bit naughty at times but there were some great characters in there who could certainly look after themselves. It was big part of me and my mates life in those days, we would go to City home and away and even though the away games brought with it the threat of violence, I loved the buzz it gave you. We would also go away with England and unfurl our Bristol City flag. The East End was our home and I spent more time with my mates in there than I did with my own family some times. We would go to games and have a ball then on an evening go to the various pubs like the Volley or the Wheatsheaf in town. Then it would be off to Vadims or the Locarno to try and get lucky. One game I do remember in the East End was against Swindon in the Littlewoods cup. We lost the first leg 3–0 up at the County Ground and there had been loads of fighting in a local pub and rumour had it that it would be payback in the return leg at Aston Gate. There was a fantastic atmosphere in the East End that night and looking around it seemed everybody was ready for trouble if it kicked off. City were winning the game 3–2 with a couple of minutes to go when all of a sudden there was a massive roar from the back of the end and everybody seemed to run out. I remember falling to the floor as people shouted, 'Its Fucking Swindon'. There was a massive fight outside and the old bill were everywhere splitting it up. I have to admit I never threw a punch, as I was more worried about the fact that I had put a hole in the Kappa jumper I had on. Afterwards we went to the pub and all laughed about it. Its a night I will always remember.

Paul 'Chick' Perry
City fan forever

I have supported City since the 1970s when I used to go to games with my dad. I remember the 1980 because that was the era when I started to go with my mates. We always stood on the East End, as that's where all the lads were. There was a certain tension in there and a real hierarchy amongst the hardnuts, not that I was one. You could see them all at the back and they were lads who had stood there since the 1970s. They all had wedge haircuts and Fila tracksuit tops. It was weird, as although you were a bit wary of them you knew that they would have your back if any trouble kicked off. I remember I used to see a lot of the lads in places like the Wheatsheaf pub or clubs like Romeo and Juliet's in the centre of Bristol and although I didn't really know them they recognised you from the East End and they would always give you a nod as a acknowledgement that you were a Eastender. I can't remember much trouble actually in the end only with the police. Most of the violence seemed to happen outside the ground and it was usually premeditated and organised by a rival firm. As far as matches go, I always loved Super Bobby Taylor and I remember a game against Huddersfield around 1988–89 seasons. We beat them 6–1 and Taylor got a hat-trick. I think Mark Gavin, Alan Walsh and I think Steve McLaren scored the other one but I might be wrong. Taylor was unplayable that day and I will always remember the east End singing 'Bob, Bob Super Bob, Bob Bob Super Bob Super Bobby Taylor'. They were great times. I don't go to games as much now as I live in Coventry but when I do go I always look at that side of the ground with affection. I will miss the East End but I hear the new stand will be fantastic.

Mark Croker
Exiled City fan

ROB NEWMAN

Throughout football many young lads have been thrown into the limelight and unfortunately sank without a trace. This could never be labelled in the direction of Bristol City's 'Captain Marvel' Rob Newman. Newman found himself in the first team more out of necessity than anything else after the Ashton eight ripped up their contracts in the fall out to the financial mess the club were in. But the lad from Bradford-on-Avon grabbed his chance with both hands and he never looked back. Happy to play in a number of roles Newman earns a reputation as jack-of-all-trades during his fledgling career. But it was in central defence that the accomplished Newman found himself at home. With his cultured passing and vision he soon progressed to Captain and led the City to Division Two in 1990 under the guidance of City boss Joe Jordan. In total Newman amassed an amazing 471 games for the Robins before he was transferred to Norwich City for £600,000 in 1991. With the Canaries he played top-flight football that he dreamed of with City. And just as he had done when he was a youngster he adapted to the step up admirably. Newman played over 200 games with Norwich before finishing his career with Southend United where he later became manager. Looking back on his City days Rob Newman's career was born out of Bristol City's darkest days and its ironic that he went onto become one of the bright lights in the side.

I was scouted by Bristol City in my local area of Bradford-on-Avon. City scout Jock Rae was the man who discovered me and he was a real gentleman. I wasn't a natural to get my apprenticeship, but I worked damn hard to try and impress the coaching staff. It obviously worked as manager Alan Dicks signed me although I'm sure I was the last one out of the eleven apprentices who signed that summer. After I had signed it was a difficult time for the club as they were falling down the leagues and in a terrible financial mess. Terry Cooper never really had much choice other than throw young lads into the side and I will always be grateful to Terry for having faith in me. The experience we gained during those times were invaluable to us as players. I was always in awe of the East End when I first started playing. The noise they produced was incredible and they were just like our 12th man. I wanted nothing more than their acceptance as I always thought they led things at Ashton Gate. I feel privileged to have been City's captain and to have led the team out at Ashton Gate is one of my great memories especially when we used to run towards the East End they used to give me Goosebumps. I am glad that I was lucky enough to have played in front of the East End like players of the past especially as they put seats in there a couple of years after I left. I wish I could of taken City into the top flight and seen Ashton Gate packed week in week out, that's probably my only regret. I still go to see the odd game now and then and I get a great response from the fans even if they do give me a bit of stick about joining Norwich City. The City fans are very dear to me and I will never forget how they made me feel welcome by giving me and the other young lads in the side time to develop as players. I will miss seeing that old stand next time I visit the Gate but I hope it signals some good times for the club.

ROB NEWMAN
BRISTOL CITY: 1981–91
APPEARANCES: 471
GOALS: 61

I have always been a regular in the East End over the years. I have always loved the atmosphere of the place. It can be funny, aggressive, explosive but never ever dull except when the seats went in. I thought long and hard about what memory to write in with and I could have picked loads as I have seen all the big matches from behind that goal, but my mates will never forgive me if I don't mention an incident that I am reminded about whenever we all get together and talk about football, whether its in the pub at work or at a party this always gets brought up so I have to share it. It was the first game of the 1982–83 season. City were in Division Four and it was a home game against Hull City. At the time City were relying on youngsters and players we generally had never heard of. I noticed a new centre-forward we had in the warm up and he looked about 5ft 5ins tall. I gave him and manager Terry Cooper loads of stick for finding this so called centre-forward from Barnsley. This got worse when a ball was played over the back of the Hull defence for this striker to run onto in front of the East End. With that he proceeded to fall over. Well I gave him terrible stick and said to everyone around me what a waste of money he was. His name was Glyn Riley and he scored later on as City won 2–0. Glyn Riley kept on scoring and became one of City's great players of the 1980s, in fact I looked it up and he scored 77 goals in 231 games. My mates and those around me never ever let me forget the stick I gave him on that opening day.

Peter Deaton
A converted Glyn Riley fan

ALAN WALSH

Alan Walsh will always be regarded by the Bristol City faithful as the best value for money player the club ever bought. The deal for the ex Darlington player went to tribunal and City's £18,000 valuation of the striker fell way below Darlington's £85,000 price tag. Incredibly the tribunal found in Bristol City's favour and one of the best deals the club had ever done was completed as Walsh put pen to paper. With his lethal left foot, Walsh would instantly become a fans favourite particularly with his dead ball skills. He would also mesmerize the fans and sometimes himself with the 'Walsh shuffle' a combination of feints and step overs. Alan was truly the gem that lay undiscovered in the lower leagues. In the four years he spent at Ashton Gate he scored 99 goals in 284 games. Always fans favourite many were devastated when he agreed a lucrative move to Turkey with Besiktas who were managed by former Coventry City manager Gordon Milne. After two league titles and a Turkish Cup under his belt Alan returned to the UK and played non-league with Clevedon Town and Taunton Town before receiving a call from his hometown club Hartlepool United for one last fling. Alan signed a years contract and he again become popular with the fans in the northeast. Unfortunately after new management at the club he found himself out of football. Fate again turned in his favour as he was offered a role at Bristol Rovers in their community department and then a place at his beloved City as part of Gary Johnson's coaching staff. Today Alan has returned to manage the Bristol Rovers under 18 squad but it will always be at Ashton Gate that this likable striker will be remembered.

I feel really honoured to be in this book and I was thrilled when Neil asked me to contribute. I have a lot of time for the Bristol City fans, they have always been good to me over the years, even now that I work for rivals Rovers. I find it really strange that I come from the North East of England and yet the people of Bristol embraced me. The areas are quite different yet I settled in the southwest immediately and that was down to the fans. The East End was a really special place to play in front of over the years. It was always the focal point of the ground and it generated some fantastic atmospheres in games over the years. I have to say that all four sides of Ashton Gate gave great support to the players but there was something special about the East End. I have loads of memories about that end of the ground and I always got a massive kick out of scoring at that end. Even if I scored the other end I would love to run back to that part of the ground to take the applause. As far as games are concerned three stick in my mind. The first one was my first goal at that end in my first season. It was the 1984–85 season and we were playing Brentford. I remember having a real tussle all game with Chris Kamara and I didn't get many chances. We had a really decent side with the likes of Bobby Hutchinson, Rob Newman, Glyn Riley and Howard Pritchard in the side. I had my back to goal and I was about 15 yards from goal when I turned and beat one Brentford defender then as I beat another I was fouled but I managed to stay on my feet and just as another defender came in to tackle me I lifted the ball over him then struck it sweetly into the top corner. It was one of the best goals I have ever scored and to get it at that end was terrific. I think we drew the game 1–1 but I loved that goal. Another memory was around 1985–86 season and it was the game against Hereford United in the Freight Rover semi-final second leg at Ashton Gate. We were 2–0 down from the first leg at Edgar Street and to be honest many people wrote us off. Except us, the players, we really thought we could score three goals in the second leg and with Ashton Gate buzzing on the night many of us thought this is it. Howard Pritchard got a deflected goal to put us 1–0 up on the night then I crossed the ball for Bobby Hutchinson to head down as Steve Neville made it 2–0. The cross was a stroke of luck really as it never really went where I wanted it to go but I never told Bobby. Soon after Stevie Neville got his second and our third as we got to Wembley 3–2. I will never forget the atmosphere that night and in particular the East End as they were incredible. My last memory was the League Cup Semi-final second leg against Nottingham Forest in 1989. It is a game that every City fan always asks me about today. We were the underdogs even though we had drawn 1–1 at the City Ground Nottingham in the first leg. It was a great atmosphere at Ashton Gate that Sunday afternoon. The TV cameras were there hoping to see Bristol City put one over on Nottingham Forest manager Brian Clough. It was a rain soaked Ashton Gate but the fans never stopped singing and giving us encouragement. To be honest we both had chances to win the game but it was hard to call who would get the edge. With about two minutes left we had a corner in front of the East End. Steve McLaren took it and City defender John Pender flicked it on towards me at the far post. I swivelled and hit it and saw it agonizingly hit the post as the whole ground held its breath. The ball spun off the post and headed towards the 'keeper with City player Rob Newman sliding in. I remember thinking go on Rob but he just couldn't reach it and a Forest defender whacked it away up field and the final whistle blew. In the extra-time that followed Forest midfielder Gary Parker got the winner for them and our dream was over. I played that incident over and over in my head. If the ball had spun a different way and crossed the line we would have been at Wembley as there was no time left for Forest to score. I get loads of City fans coming up to me today saying they were in the East End that day and they had their hearts in their mouths. I will miss the old East End, but I like many players and supporters will always have the memories of games and incidents around it.

ALAN WALSH
BRISTOL CITY: 1984–89
APPEARANCES: 284
GOALS: 99

Many great memories of standing in the East End watching games. I thought long and hard before writing in. There were so many memories of that part of the ground. The great thing about the place was that it felt like the centre of all things Bristol City. It was where the chants started, it were all the gossip about the club took place, it was where you would find the latest fashion and lads would know the latest boozers and clubs to go in. There are too many games to pick one out, but my everlasting memory would be the atmosphere the place generated. Especially on night games it was something really special. I am glad that I experienced the East End, as I moved when they put seats in and it broke my heart when they let away supporters have a section of it. I wont miss the toilets, as they were something else. I took my girlfriend once and she needed the loo. Lets just say she never wanted to set foot in the place ever again. I am looking forward to seeing the plans for the new stand but I will never forget the old East End and the memories that came with it.

Paul Hagan

I started to go to watch City in the late 1960s with my dad. My favourite player at the time was John Galley. I used to go on my own with my mates around 1975. We would always go to the East End as it was where most of our mates from school would be. I thought long and hard about different games to remember and they are all etched into my brain for life. Cup wins, Relegations, promotions, they all surround the East End. But the one thing I remember takes me back to the 1980s about 1985 to be precise. In the summer months me and my mates used to go down to Ashton Gate on a Thursday night for keep fit. You could pay £5 and that entitled you to get changed in the away changing room, use the sauna and run around the outside of the pitch. We would go and run into Long Ashton and back then do four laps of the pitch before running up and down the steps of the Dolman stand. At the end of the session I would always make a point of opening the gate to the East End and resting on the concrete step before I went inside and had my shower. I will never forget the feeling I got when I used to sit in the ground when there was nobody in it and the East End became almost church like. We did this through the summer months before City, for some reason stopped doing it. Those summer evenings sat alone on the steps of the terrace will always be magical as far as I am concerned and that will be my lasting memory of that great area of the ground.

Rick Smith
City fan

The game for me has got to be the Freight Rover semi-final second leg at Ashton Gate. I have been a City fan since the 1970s and my place at the ground was always the East End. Like so many fans I have seen some incredible games, players and incidents from those terraces over the years. The Portsmouth game when we won promotion on that lovely warm evening is obviously up there but like I said before It's the Hereford game that stays in my mind. I know the Portsmouth match meant everything to us as we had reached the First Division and the thought of playing all those top teams like Arsenal, Liverpool and Leeds United was incredible. But I will never forget the feeling that overcame me when I realized that we had got to Wembley. It was a fantastic night and the East End was jam packed from early on. We trailed 2–0 from the first leg but there was something about that night it was special. The East End never stopped singing and the tension that ran through the terraces as we clawed our way back to win 3–2 was electric. When Steve Neville got the winner we all just exploded with joy. I remember the players went mental and we just joined them. It was a special night to be a City fan.

Alan Ford
Bristol City fan

I used to love going to the East End in the 1980s. It was an incredible place and looking back on it we were lucky to of experienced it. I know it had a fierce some reputation in the 1970s and 80s but with the seats going in and the away

fans being put in there I'm glad I can say I stood on that
terracing when it was a proper end. The toilets were shit
and you could smell them over the tea hut, but looking
back they were great days. I would see people and chat to
them even though I really knew nothing about their lives
only that they supported City. I would see lads in the Naval
Volunteer or the Hatchet in town and we would nod or
say hello and that was only because I saw them in the
East End. If there was any trouble in pubs in town I would
have their backs and they would have mine due to the fact
that they were City fans. I remember getting pulled out by
some coppers once and getting nicked for being drunk and
pissing against the back wall. I think the game was against
Tranmere Rovers. I must have been the only one who ever
got caught doing it. I remember pissing on the coppers leg
as I turned round to face him before he threw me out. I
don't think there will be any of that in the new stand. I'm
looking forward to a new era for City and the redevelopment of the ground looks amazing.

Shaun Kelly
City Fan

What about the game against Nottingham Forest in the
League Cup semi-final second leg. I remember it was pissing down with rain all day and it was on ITV. Nobody gave
us much of a chance but as the game went on you could
see the East End and the players growing in confidence. I
remember Alan Walsh hitting the post in the last minute
and we all jumped on top of each other as we thought it

was in. We did not mind the rain during the game but after Forest scored in extra-time it ruined our day especially the walk home to Knowle. We were soaking wet and freezing. If only Alan had put it in.

Paul Irons

I remember going to Ashton Gate for the first time in the 1980s to see the Rolling Stones. I can't remember what year but I think it was 1986. I went with some of my friends from work. We just wanted to see Mick Jagger and apparently we were in the East End. I heard they were doing a book on that part of the ground and I had to check with my son who goes to City if that's where I saw the Stones. I wanted to contribute, as people still don't believe me when I tell them my one and only time at Ashton Gate was watching the Rolling Stones.

Julie Williams

I have always been a City fan as I come from south Bristol so it was only ever going to be the reds for me. I have been to hundreds of games spanning the 1960s, 70s and 80s and they were when I used to go in the East End. It had a real reputation for trouble which to be honest was well deserved. My memory revolves around the terrace when there was nobody in it. In the 1980s I was working for a delivery company called RG Merchants. They were based in Filton Bristol and I covered the entire southwest delivering anything from Paint to fridges. I got a job delivering some packages to Ashton Gate, which I must admit was the highlight of my day. I remember going to the main reception and after delivering the packages I asked the girl in reception if I could go into the ground. She agreed and I walked around the back of the East End and went onto the terraces and had my sandwiches. Its really funny but I will always remember that hour I spent watching the grounds man work. It was surreal to be in a place that was jam packed when I went there on a Saturday. It just shows the affection I have for the place that I should remember that dinner break. I will miss the place when it gets pulled down although I can see the need for change. I hope my memory however brief is worthy of the book

Ken Thorley

If I had to pick a memory about the East End it would be the 1980s. This was my era of going in there. I first went to City with my dad in the 1970s and we used to stand on the terraces in front of the Williams stand. These were the days of the First Division and we saw all the top sides then. The East End was a real hard old place and I was always fascinated by it on match days. It was noisy and I remember the fans never seemed to stop singing. My dad and all their mates used to say that all the 'nut jobs' went in there but that made it even more fascinating too me. At school you would find that as lads got older they progressed away from watching games with their dads and inevitably went to the East End with their mates and I was no exception. I can remember the first game I ever went to with my mates from school in the East End and it was the opening game of the 1984–85 season against Wigan Athletic. I was shitting myself to be honest as I was 14 years old and there I was in amongst blokes that looked like lunatics but once the singing started and the game kicked off I was completely hooked on the place. City won the game 2–0 with goals from Glyn Riley and I have never ever enjoyed myself so much. I look back and it seems like a right of passage for me as from that moment on I think I started to rely less on my mum and dad and I started to hang about with older lads. I will miss the East End when they pull it down.

Pete Kavanagh

I hope my memory of the East End is good enough to put in this book. I think the idea is great and I can't wait to read other fans stories when it comes out. My memory is of the last game of the 1989–90 season. City had won promotion from League Three to League Two. They finished the season in second place but I won't mention who finished top. We were regulars in the East End and this game was a celebration of our promotion. We played Walsall and City was head and shoulders above them. City were 4–0 up with about 10 minutes to go and all the fans got onto the pitch in anticipation of running on the pitch to celebrate. More and more fans came onto the pitch as the game carried on and in the end you could not see the white lines of the touchline, as it was now a wall of people. Me and my mates had got out from the East End and were actually leaning against the goal post with the poor old Walsall 'keeper stood next to us. City had a shot and the ball fell to myself and I picked it up and at that moment the ref blew his whistle and all the fans ran on as the players ran off. This left me with the ball still in my hands so I kept it. I carried it for a few moments and the fans never paid it any attention, as we were all celebrating promotion. I stayed for a bit then went home along with the ball. Today it sits in my house on top of a wardrobe and it always brings back memories of that great afternoon in and out of the East End.

Kenny Moorland

My first game in the East End was in 1983–84 season. It was against Mansfield and we won 4–0. I went to the game with my mates and I was always a City fan, but I had never been in the East End. I went with some older lads and it was great you really felt like you were part of a family. That feeling never left me and I always-preferred going in the East End as it was 'our end'. There was always trouble and I think that added to the excitement when you're young. As you get older you concentrate on the game yet when I was younger I was more interested in the opposition fans and singing all the songs. I loved the place and I along with a lot of my friends will miss it. It wont be the same driving along Winterstoke Road and not seeing it there anymore.

Andy Thomas
City Fan

I was an East End regular through the 1970s and the 80s. I changed when they put the seats in and I went into the Dolman with my kids. I loved going and in particular standing behind the goal and giving rival fans and players stick. I remember one such incident when City were playing Aston Villa in the FA Cup. The date was about 1981 and Villa were in the top flight and City were in the Third Division. All through the half we gave Villa 'keeper Jimmy Rimmer stick. We called him every name under the sun. Villa won the game 1–0. At the final whistle he turned to us in the East End dropped his shorts a bit and showed us all the jock strap he was wearing. Everybody jeered and to be honest I'm surprised he never got done by the FA. Maybe he would have if it was on TV. I laughed and thought it was funny and it just typifies the East End for me. It was a funny and intimidating place to be in and I loved every minute of it. I will miss it.

Dan Gomerby

The 1980s were a strange decade for the club. It started with the club battling for survival and ended with the club pushing for promotion. In 1982 the club were on their backside financially and they offered a fantastic deal on season tickets in the Dolman stand that worked out cheaper than standing on the East End. A lot of lads took that opportunity to move out of the East End and many stayed there right up until today creating their own atmosphere in the Dolman. The football violence was still with us and I remember a game against Millwall at Ashton Gate that was the worse football violence I had ever seen at the Gate. Many fans fell out of love for that sort of stuff that day especially the lads who were about from the 1960s.

Tom Hopegood
City Fan

6.

THE NINETIES

The 1990s started as a decade of optimism with the fall of the Berlin wall and the subsequent end of the 'Cold war' as we knew it. After the excess of the eighties the early nineties would predictably mean recession for the UK. Caused by high interest rates combined with falling house prices and a overvalued exchange rate that caused a rise in the mortgage rate, there were some tough times ahead as people struggled to keep hold of their houses. The country saw a need for change after Conservative governments and Labours leader Tony Blair tapped into the voters need for change and in 1997 he found himself in Number 10 with a promise to look after the average working man or Mondeo man as he put it. As the decade advanced Blair also tackled the historically difficult problem of Northern Ireland and at the end of the decade he managed to get all parties around the table to thrash out the Northern Ireland peace process. A process that resulted in both the IRA and the Loyalists laying down their arms to move the country forward. In Bristol the Imperial tobacco or (Wills Building as it was known) was closed in Hartcliffe as production was moved to Nottingham. Despite this there was money invested in City projects as we climbed out of recession. The benefactors were places like the City dock where apartments and restaurants started to spring up where once stood warehouses. This was the same for the south of the river where money had started to be spent regenerating the Bedminster area of the City that had been so neglected through the 1970s and 80s after the Wills company had pulled out of the area. Bristol as a whole was starting to grow culturally as music bands such as Massive Attack, Roni Size, Portishead and Tricky developed 'The Bristol Sound' which had its roots from the multi cultural society that Bristol was becoming. This gained worldwide recognition along with former Punk and graffiti artists Banksy and Inky creating a movement that still exists today. On the terraces fashion was just as important and along with bands such as Oasis and Blur, dance music and the rave scene became a massive part of terrace life along with the drugs ecstasy and cocaine, which became the recreational drug of choice for some fans.

For the national game the decade would be the most important for domestic football for years. British clubs were allowed back into European competitions culminating in Manchester United winning the European Champions League at the end of the decade. It was also the time when people fell back in love with the game, some even referred to it as 'Footie'. The love affair started back in Italy with Italia 90 as England under Bobby Robson valiantly lost on penalties to the Germans in the World Cup Semi-final. England and particularly Robson were given no chance in the lead up to the Finals but as the momentum grew on the pitch so did the support back home as fans fell in love with Gazzas tears and over 50,000 fans met the team when they arrived back in the UK. This passion for the national team carried on through Euro 96 when England held the European Championships. Again given a hard time in the lead up by the press Terry Venables side lost again on penalties to Germany in the semi-finals. But as the nation sung along with Baddiel and Skinner *Footballs Coming Home* football was it seemed at last back in the hearts of the nation. Many changes took place in the 1990s including the implementation of the Taylor Report following the Hillsborough tragedy as clubs started to build new stadiums and modernise the old ones. Many fans thought of the impending changes to their grounds as cultural vandalism but for others the changes could not come soon enough. Early in the decade we would see the introduction of the Premier League with its input from SKY TV and all the money it would bring. Early changes saw the end of the traditional 3pm kick-off on a Saturday as games kicked off all over the week and weekend at different times so to fit in with TV scheduling. One of the biggest changes to the game was made by the European Court of Justice in 1995 as a run-of-the-mill midfielder from Belgium club Club DE Liege wanted to move to French club Dunkerque. His name was Jean-Marc Bosman and the courts decision would change the game worldwide forever. Bosman signed a two-year deal with Liege. On its expiry his new deal offered by the club would reduce his wages by 60%. French Club Dunkerque offered a potential solution but their valuation of Bosman fell well below Liege asking price so Bosman had to stay with the Belgium club. He therefore took the club to court stating that in European law workers were free to move between member's states for employment. The court found in his favour and this meant that players became bosses of their own contract. It would also mean that players whose contracts had run out were due the 'transfer fee' in terms of a signing on fee and they could negotiate their own salaries with buying clubs. The revolution affected players who were already contracted as they wanted pay parity with their colleagues and it would also mean that players could arrive from all over the world to sign for clubs. This move also saw the emergence of agents as they represented player's interest in negotiations and sometimes sought to move players to other clubs whether they had asked for a transfer or not. Due to this they became the lowest of the low for some fans and it's a tag they have carried ever since. For supporters as a whole they were treated to a steady stream of the worlds best players such as Eric Cantona, Gianfranco Zola and Dennis Bergkamp who plied their trade in the Premier League and although fans felt detached from players at their clubs, due to money, they had more of a voice with the new culture in Football Fanzines, Football Forums and Talk radio shows, all of which gave supporters a chance to let off steam regarding footballing issues of the day.

As for Bristol City the decade would see the start of the death of the East End as it was known. Changes were afoot as it was renamed the Wedlock stand after ex player Billy Wedlock and seats were installed. For the faithful the last indignation was the move for away fans to be given part of the end. This move would see many supporters move to other areas of the ground. Many by choice as they felt the atmosphere would not be what it once was. There were other changes at the ground as a new stand was built on the site of the open end and called the Atyeo stand which was a fitting tribute to former great John Atyeo who died in 1993. On the pitch the club struggled to find some consistency regarding the managers hot seat as they started the decade with Joe Jordan and went through Jimmy Lumsden, Dennis Smith, Russell Osman, Joe Jordan, John Ward, Benny Lennartsson, Tony Pulis and Tony Fawthorpe with only John

Ward bringing any kind of success with promotion to Division One in the 1997–98 season. The club spent one season in the division before being relegated back to Division Two where they remained until the end of the decade. Although it was not the greatest of decades for the club the various managers employed at least brought some players to the club that supporters would never forget, Players like Darius Dziekanowski a mercurial polish international who was signed from Celtic who outwitted and outclassed many opponents. Although he only spent two seasons at the club his skill and ability to put fans on the edge of their seats will never be forgotten. Another was Andy Cole who came initially on loan from Arsenal. You could tell that this goalscorer was never going to be at the City long even though manager Denis Smith signed him for £500,000. Again he never stayed long before being sold to Newcastle United for £1.75 million scoring 25 goals in 49 games for the Robins. There was also Scott Murray who joined from Aston Villa in 1997 and never looked back. A player who gave everything for the club. Add to the list Shaun Goater who's goals helped secure promotion in the 1997–98 season and local lads Tommy Doherty who's never say die attitude in midfield reminded older fans of a certain 1970s legend Gerry Gow and Louis Carey who played beyond his years at the heart of the defence. And not forgetting a Geordie with one of the best left foots ever seen at Ashton Gate in Brian Tinnion. Off the pitch the club also recruited a new board member in the shape of local businessman Stephen Lansdown in 1996. With him at the helm the future looked rosy as we came into the new millennium.

Being a season ticket holder and a City fan for more than 30 years the memory that sticks in my mind is when a friend (Jason Jones) and me got tickets for the 1990 FA Cup clash with Chelsea at Ashton Gate, having secured a great position behind the East End goal, the game commenced in a fast pace and it wasn't long before City forced Chelsea goalkeeper Dave Beasent into an error which enabled City forward Robbie Turner a chance to put us 1–0 up. In the euphoria of the fans the East End erupted, it seemed like we jumped 10ft high, but in the process my friends glasses were knocked off and this subsequently meant he watched the remainder of the game with blurred vision. However this did not dampen his spirits as I gave him a running commentary and going on to win 3–1 was probably one of the best results I have ever witnessed as a guide dog.

Paul Fletch Martin
City Fan

I don't have many memories of the East End as it is or was. I have been a regular in the Atyeo for the last 15 years, and as a kid and non-season ticket holder I stand-hopped a lot.

I don't have many exciting stories, but I do remember one visit to the East End around Christmas during John Wards time in charge. I think it was against Watford and a new signing had just come off the bench to make his home debut for us. Just along from me a couple of young blokes were chatting and after a few minutes of watching this player, who had come on as a sub and consequently fluffed a cross, asked each other who he was? "He's our new signing from Villa, Murray I think." "We bought him?" "How much did we pay?" "About £250,000" "Well I hope John Ward kept the receipt".

As it turned out that was one of the finest £250,000 we have spent in the last quarter of a century. But it goes to show how quick people are to judge sometimes. When someone's been around forever, you get used to them and call them a legend, forgetting their flaws. Hopefully not too many people will rush to judge the new stand but will give it time to bed in, get used to it, and appreciate it.

Mat Rees
City fan

I first made my trip down to the West Country in the early 90s for a game against Tranmere Rovers. We set off excited and eager to get to Ashton Gate. Aged just 18 this was my first trip to the Gate and not knowing what to expect having supported the club and only having gone to a few away games mainly at Coventry. This was it! A 187-mile round trip to see the club I had grown to love at Ashton Gate which now holds so many memories. Having arrived at the Gate we went to get the tickets. Which stand to choose? The Williams? Or shall we stand? It looks like rain said my mate so let's go in the East End plus its a pound cheaper (my mate was right, cheap git). But how glad I was that we picked the East End. We entered the stand and I was like a kid in a sweetshop for the very first time. No backs on the seats, it did not matter no food kiosk in the middle it did not matter, toilets with huge queues it did not matter this was it, I'm at the Gate I'm in the East End, I'm watching Bristol City. Then near 3pm the stands starts filling up and fans start chatting and they realise I am not from the west country but from the midlands (Leamington spa) and the start of some great friendships begin and still last to this day some 22 years later. The game finished 2–2 but in a way the result did not matter as I was here at Ashton Gate in the East End.

Then it happened, I discovered beer and a pre-match drink or two was required, The Robins? Nice pub, but not for me. Where next? Ship and Castle, great pub but then what's that we see? Wedlock's Pub the place to be for any City supporter before the game. Over the years I have spent many Saturdays on the East End. I have cried tears of joy at promotions, shed tears of disappointment at relegations and have continued to have friendship of over 20 years which all began in the East End. More than just a stand, it's more a way of life being a Bristol City fan.

Duncan James

I took my daughter Lily to her first match, aged four, against Millwall where City squandered a 2–0 lead only to be pegged back to 2–2 by the time the final whistle blew. Not that she was bothered by this having chosen to make the family enclosure, then situated in the corner of the East End, as her own personal playground and spent most of the second half skipping up and down the terraced concrete steps quite happily whilst I watched with one eye on the game and one on her. Football and City became part of my daughter's life. Lily played for the Robins, from five years old until she turned 13, and we moved away to Cornwall. I was duly 'roped in' to help with training and eventually manage one of the girl's teams and I have many great memories of her playing and both of us watching City together.

It was on one occasion, a few years later, as we sat in the East End, standing had ended the year before lily's spectator debut, whilst watching an unmemorable game that Lily turned to me and asked a question about City playing some of the top flights big teams. I replied that she was talking about the Premiership. "Are we Premiership Daddy?" "No Lilly we are League One." There was a confused look on her face, and as little was happening in the game, with both teams at stalemate, the next ten minutes or so was taken up explaining the rigours of the English league system and how teams were promoted and relegated. Lily thought of this for a while, her face frowning in concentration as we both watched over the dire spectacle opening up before us. Suddenly she turned and looked up at me. "Daddy will we ever be Premiership?"

I looked at her little face, eyes now wide, a beautiful picture of optimism. I thought for a moment how to watch City will give you a lesson in life, taking you through all the emotions, the highs, lows, dissapointments, frustration and yes optimism. Without the latter we would be nothing, but how to answer? I thought carefully and it seemed like minutes past in those fleeting seconds. Certainly nothing had happened on the pitch. Hope needed to spring eternal and so I answered with as much conviction as possible 'One day sweetheart, one day.'

My daughter listened to this, but continued to hold my gaze whilst contemplating my answer. Football grounds are noisy affairs for the most part and even this mid-season, nothing to play for affair, which it seemed had the heart wrung out of it was only kept alive by the fans providing defibrillation as they sung their chants, songs and calls of encouragement in a vain attempt to spark the life back in their team. I swear for one moment it seemed to hush as lily looked straight into my eyes and said..."That means never Daddy doesn't it?"

Alec Rice
City Fan

I have always loved being in the East End, I have always thought of it as the 'heart' of the ground. It always creates the atmosphere that generates all around the rest of the terraces. I remember a cold January night in the East End around 1992. In front of me and my mates were three lads with green and white scarf's just poking out of their thick jackets. They were looking all around the East End and it was obvious that they had never been in the ground before. This really intrigued me as we were playing Southend United and they did not play in green and white. We were one nil down at half-time and one of the guys went to the toilets and the call of nature just so happened to coincide with my own need for the loo. We got chatting and I discovered that the three lads were Celtic fans and had come down from Glasgow to see City's new signing 'Jackie' Dziekanowski. They explained that he was a legend at Celtic due to him scoring four goals in one of the most incredible nights ever seen at Celtic Park. It was a UEFA Cup match and Partizan Belgrade were the opposition. The Yugoslavs team were 2–1 winners in the first leg in Belgrade so Celtic had it all to do in the second leg. Jackie scored four goals as Celtic won 5–4 on the night but went out on away goals. The Celtic fans loved him from that night. Back in Bristol on that cold January night City drew 2–2 with Jackie getting one of City's goals. My mates and I went drinking with the Scottish lads till well into the night and they have become great friends ever since with us venturing up to Scotland on many occasions. We both shared our love for one of City's and Celtics greats and we met in the East End.

Paul Tilden
City fan

My favourite memory of the East End goes back to the 1991–92 season. I was 14 years old and I went to watch the City for the first time with some friends from school. It was a night game against Wolverhampton Wanderers. I remember City were on a bit of a losing streak and new manager Dennis Smith had just taken over. We had not won for eight games and with the game at 0–0 with about five minutes left at least we looked like we were going to get a point. Dennis Smith threw Jackie Dziekanowski on from the subs bench and he went on to score two goals which saved our season. I remember the East End went mental and it was rocking even when the players left the pitch after the final whistle, we just did not want to go home. It was a fantastic night.

Matty Reybold
City fan for 30 years

My fondest memory of being in the East End was the Wolves game in the early 1990s. Dennis Smith was manager and we could not buy a win. We were near the bottom of the table and drawing 0–0 when he sent on Jackie Dziekanowski for the last ten minutes of the game and he scored two goals. The East End went crazy that night. I will never forget it.

Graham Adams
Lockleaze

BRIAN TINNION

Brian Tinnion was brought up watching his beloved Newcastle United from their famous Gallowgate end at St James's Park. As with most young lads who follow their team young Tinnion dreamed of pulling on the black and white stripes of his heroes and running out on the St Jamess' park pitch. Tinnion achieved this along with close friend and fellow Geordie Paul Gascoigne under the watchful eye of manager Jack Charlton. Both youngsters were tipped for great things but whereas Gascoigne's 'crash and burn' career is well documented young Brian had to move away from the North east to get regular football after a management upheaval at the club which saw Jack Charlton leave. The young Tinnion found himself at Bradford City where he became fans favourite but with his contract nearing its end he was given an opportunity to join Bristol City under John Ward. Brian made his City debut in a West Country derby against Swindon Town and although City lost 2–1 a love affair with a club was about to start. Brian made over 450 appearances for the club and scored 42 goals including the winner in a famous FA Cup win against Liverpool at Anfield. Nearing the end of his career he was offered the managerial hot seat at Ashton Gate the morning after City's gutless defeat against Brighton in the 2004 Play-off Final at the Millennium Stadium Cardiff. Brian took the job and although his only experience of coaching was working with the kids at City's academy on the evenings he took City to seventh position in his first season. Brian was never afraid to give youngsters a chance and this would, along with a crippling injury list, be his downfall as City went to Swansea City and were hammered 7–1 severn games into the 2005–06 season. Brian resigned and although chairman Stephen Lansdown begged him to stay Tinnion left the club and was given an opportunity to run soccer schools for Charlton Athletic in Spain. He also hooked up with ex City player David Moyes who asked him to become Everton's European Scout. But the pull of Ashton Gate proved to be too strong and Brian returned to Bristol to become Head of Recruitment at Bristol City's Academy based in Filton. Tinnion will always be one of the icons of the nineties regarding Bristol City. He was a player who could send a killer pass with his left foot and with his skill he could dictate the pace of the game from midfield. Many players have worn the red shirt of City but not many have given there all like Tinnion on and off the pitch.

I simply love the club. When I was a kid I used to stand on the Gallowgate end watching Newcastle United and the noise was incredible, so I'm not joking when I say that Bristol City's East End used to give me the same Goosebumps. I loved the support of all the fans at Ashton Gate but I knew the hardcode City fans were in that end and they made the most noise. I felt at the tim, like lots of players, that we lost something when they put the away fans in it especially when we were in the championship as there were some big clubs in that league and they all had a good following. I suppose it was how I was brought but I always thought a club should have their own end. The City fans have been very good too me over the years, I loved running out to their applause and to get a goal in front of the East End was a special moment for me. Even if I scored at the other end I would always run to the East End if I could. They made you feel as though they could suck the ball into the oppositions net. As I said the club are very special too me so when I got the call to manage them I really could not turn it down. I always think that you only regret things that you say no to not the things you say yes to. In hindsight, yes maybe I should of left the club and got some experience somewhere else or maybe become a number two as I did not have a lot of experience, but looking back plenty of managers have come to Ashton Gate with big reputations and failed to deliver so I don't think I did that bad. I finished seventh and just out of the play-offs in my first season and I started a lot of young lads' careers by giving them their chance in the side, lads like Dave Cottrell and Leroy Lita who would all go on and be sold for a profit.

Trouble is people forget that and only concentrate on that one afternoon at The Vetch, Swansea when an understrength City side got hammered 7–1. It seems that result has defined my managerial career at the club, which is a bit unfair. When I left I took up an opportunity to set up some soccer schools in Spain and I was also working for Everton looking at La Liga games for them. The family were happy and so was I. In fact I swore I would never come back, but then I got a call from the club and it was another job that I could not turn down. I was offered head of recruitment, which meant that I was responsible for lads from 8–21. It was a chance to shape the future of this great club. I spoke at length with Mr Lansdown about his vision for the club and although the scouting network was in disarray when I joined I could see that the club had progressed off the field in leaps and bounds in terms of infrastructure. Stephen Lansdown told me that he would love to see 11 lads from Bristol playing for the club and although that's probably not ever going to happen in the modern game the sentiment is right. We aim to stop local lads signing for clubs like Southampton, Aston Villa, WBA, Cardiff City and Swansea City who all operate in the area and we want lads to sign because we do things right rather than any loyalty to the club. As I said the club is moving forward and with the new improvements to Ashton Gate it will be even easier to show a youngster and his parents around the club with a view to signing. I miss the East End but I will always have that memory of those supporters chanting my name through thick and thin when I was a player and the manager. It's those sorts of memories that made me return to this club and hopefully help shape its future. People often ask me if I would like to return to management one day, but I feel I have one of the most important jobs at the club and I am incredibly proud to be associated with the club again.

BRIAN TINNION
BRISTOL CITY: 1992–05
APPEARENCES: 497
GOALS: 42

I will always remember the Coca-Cola cup game against Cardiff when we beat them 5–1 at Ashton Gate. Andy Cole was on fire that night and he scored a hat-trick. I was in the East End as usual and although they had put seats in it I never moved from my spot off to the right hand side as you walked in. I will be sad to see it go, but I suppose we all still have the memories.

Mike Davis

SCOTT MURRAY

There are few City players who have been taken into the hearts of City supporters like Scott Murray has. Especially after leaving the club at what was thought the height of his career, but when he returned he became even more loved by the City following. Arriving from Aston Villa in 1997–98 season Murray would turn out to be one of the best match winners the clubs supporters had ever seen. Great ability, pace and and a good touch saw Murray terrorize defences throughout his time at the club. Born in Aberdeen, Murray played part-time Highland League football for Fraserborough before fending off the challenges of Rangers to sign for Aston Villa. Struggling to gain a first team place at the club he was snapped up by City manager John Ward for the 97–98 promotion push. Murray went from strength to strength with the Robins scoring 26 goals in the 2002–03 seasons. That summer he was chased by Reading Football Club who offered City £650,000 for his signature. City agreed although those that had watched him week in and out thought the valuation way under what City could have got. Scott's time at Reading saw him homesick and in and out of the side before being brought back in 2003–2004 by City manager Danny Wilson. Scott renewed his love affair with the City fans scoring 69 goals in 277 games for the club. He is still a popular figure amongst City players and supporters as he is now the clubs kit man.

When I arrived at Bristol City I did not know much about Bristol if I'm honest. I remember coming to the ground and thinking that it looked a bit like Aberdeen's ground. Not just because it was all red but it looked about the right size. It was a really big move for me. I had been playing part-time in the Highland League whilst working as a fork lift truck driver and I was earning more money doing that than I was at Aston Villa but I always wanted to be a footballer so, when John Ward came in for me I knew I might get a regular game and that was what I wanted. It is really difficult for many City players of my generation to talk about The Wedlock Stand as when I played it was certainly not the end that City supporters would talk to me about when they referred to it as the East End. It now had seats in and away supporters. I know they made hell of a noise in that part of the ground and I can only imagine what it was like in its hey day back in the 60s, 70s, and 80s. I have always had a great rapport with the City fans and I loved hugging the touchline in front of the Dolman and Williams stand as I could hear every word they said although sometimes I would rather not hear what they said when we were loosing. Its funny but I loved celebrating at the Wedlock End, as I said it was always about the noise that part of the ground created. I have had some great times at the City and the supporters have meant a lot to me. When I left for Reading I wasn't really that keen on going and I was overjoyed when the City got me back and supporters treated me as though I had never been away. I will always be grateful to them for that. When I look to the future its great to still be part of the club that I care about and with the new stand and things falling into place off the field it looks like there is more success to come and I hope to be part of it.

SCOTT MURRAY
BRISTOL CITY: 1997–98, 2002–03 and 2003–04
APPEARANCES: 277
GOALS: 69

7.

INTO THE MILLENIUM AND BEYOND

So as we enter the millennium and beyond we find the world a much different place than at the end of the nineties. Terrorism on a global scale has changed our lives after the wars in Iraq and Afghanistan. These events have changed our lives in terms of travel forever and the explosion of the internet and social media has changed the way we communicate, with not only each other, but with the whole world. Bristol has become the Green Capital of Europe and extensive investment in the region has meant that not only is it one of the most expensive places to live outside London, but it was also recently voted the second most desirable place to live outside the capital.

For the national game we see the Premier League going from strength to strength with the average player earning £42,000 a week. We have seen a huge influx in foreign players and managers, which has certainly affected our national team as it has lurched from one World Cup disaster to the next during the last 15 years. We currently have 32% of players playing in the Premier League who are not English compared to just eleven players in 1992–93 at the Premier Leagues inception. The Millennium and subsequent years have effectively marked the death of the East End as it was remembered in the chapters of this book. The decline has not been that of neglect on Bristol City's part but the continuation of The Taylor report. The change started with the installation of seats at the end, a move that although not popular with some fans they could at least see why, due to the tragedy's at various stadiums in the 1980s. The whole dynamics of Ashton Gate changed in 1995 with the opening of the Atyeo stand on the site of the old open end. This allowed away supporters to to be given part of the East End or Wedlock stand as it was now called. This proved to be the final death knell for some of the hard-core fans as they moved to different parts of the ground citing that it would never be the same. Prior to the announcement that the club were going to redevelop the south part of Ashton Gate there had been seven long years of wrangling between the club, Bristol City Council, various action groups, residents and green activist's regarding chairman Stephen Lansdowns vision to build a new state of the art stadium at nearby Ashton Vale. The clubs defeat on this project could have made a lesser chairman walk away from the club, but Lansdown has committed himself not only to Bristol City's future but the future of Bristol sport in general. After going back to the drawing board the club submitted plans to renovate the Wedlock and Williams stand. On the pitch the club have experienced football in the third tier of footballs pyramid and also found themselves 90 minutes away from a place in the Premier League. Managers have come and gone, some experienced and some not, this can also be said for players. There has been a LDV Final in Cardiff and a couple of JPT Finals at Wembley along with the odd promotion and relegation thrown in for good measure.

And so 26 April 2014 as the final whistle went in the 0–0 draw with Crewe Alexandra the structure at the south end of Ashton Gate that was known to fans throughout the pages of this book as The covered end, The East End and The Wedlock End was no more. In its place will be a brand new structure that will be state of the art for the modern fan with a capacity of 6,071 and will take Ashton Gate into a 27,000 all seater stadium. Whatever the future holds for football, Bristol City and for the fans that will take their seats in the new structure, the past belongs to the voices and the footsteps of the old terrace, some of which have been recorded in the pages of this book. There would be no stand; no Bristol City had families over the generations not made the East End their home. That continuity, traced by peoples footsteps and stitched with people's dreams, is lifeblood to the sense of tradition that has made Bristol City what it is today. Lose that the sense of who we are and where we have been – and we lose the thread we need to secure our football future. The new stand will be the home on which supporters will form their own new memories, who knows maybe we will see a volume two of *Behind the Goal* in 100 years time... With maybe a different author.

I am glad the club have decided to knock down the old East End. The condition of some grounds around the country including that part of Ashton Gate is shocking. Clubs need to provide fans with better facilities in which to watch games. We need better seats, better toilets, better food. I think its long overdue and in a few years time fans will wonder what all the fuss was about.

Mike Graham
City fan for over 50 years.

We had to grow up from the terraces. I mean we were second-class citizens, really. Obviously facilities had improved, but not that much. I suppose when you are younger you don't know any different or you can't afford a seat.

Tony Gill
City fan

I have stood and sat in the East End since the 1970s I will be sad to see it go. I have had many memories over the years in that part of the ground, but I will never forget the very last game against Crewe. It was a magical atmosphere, just like the good old days. I don't mind admitting that I shed a tear for the old girl as we left and I wasn't the only one.

Peter Wild
City till I die

I remember the play-off semi-final against Crystal Palace the roof nearly came off. It was a very special night and one I will remember for a long time. The thought that we were going to Wembley and were going to be one game away from the Premier League was fantastic. I remember walking home and getting some chips. The whole chip shop in Bedminster was singing. I never slept all night with excitement and I'm 46 years old.

Adam Winsor

I used to go to games in the East End throughout the 70s and 80s. When I got kids I moved to the Dolman Stand and I have stayed ever since with my sons. But there was no way I was missing the last game against Crewe. I couldn't get tickets for my sons, but I got one and I was determined to say one last goodbye to the East End as I know it the atmosphere was great and I saw loads of my old muckers in the pubs around the ground beforehand. Loads of the lads had the same idea and had got tickets. It was a terrible game but we just sang all the old songs and if I'm honest I felt really upset at the end. I went back when they started to demolish it and I got a brick for my garden that I have painted red. I always touch it for good luck when I'm off too Ashton Gate to see City.

Davey Adams
City Fan

When I heard about this book I thought long and hard about a memory from the East End. I like many before me always used the East End growing up through the 70s and 80s. I have had some great times there with my mates but one memory I will always cherish was in 2007 when we clinched promotion to the Championship. I stopped going into the East End during the late 90s when I thought it lost a bit of its sparkle in terms of atmosphere. I moved to the Dolman Stand. I remember getting some tickets from work for the last game of the season against Rotherham. We needed a result to clinch promotion under Gary Johnson. The tickets included some for kids so I took my two sons who were six and eight years old. I admit that it wasn't the same in the end especially as we were now sat down but it was wonderful to celebrate with my kids as City won 3–1. When I look back it was fitting that I should enjoy the game with my kids in a place where I had grown up watching City. So it will have to be the Rotherham game for me even though they cost me a fortune in food!

Dave Gingell
Ashton

I remember being in the Wedlock stand for the semi-final Play-off game against Hartlepool. It was an incredible night for atmosphere and to their credit the Hartlepool supporters played their part in making the noise. I could feel the whole place shake and when Christian Roberts scored the winner I thought the roof was going to come off the Wedlock. It was certainly one of those nights that as a supporter you never forget and gives you goosebumps just talking about it.

Pete Sealy
Midsomer Norton

I have been supporting Bristol City from 1968 home and away. If I had to pick a memory for this book it would be the last game at the East End against Crewe Alexander. A lot of the young kids who went to the game never really understood what a big part that terrace played in blokes lives watching City, as it was always the place to be. When the game ended there were blokes like me in their late forties just standing looking at the pitch. We just nodded to each other, as we knew how we felt about the end of an era for us. I could feel myself welling up inside when I looked around. I remember going to a couple of pubs in Bedminster that night and just chatting about things we did on the East End. I think the book is a great idea.

Tony Fletcher
Hartcliffe

I hope my memory is ok for the book. It has to be that last night game, watching City from the East End against Port Vale. I moved out of the East End when the seats went in and I moved to the Dolman Stand but I was not going to miss the last night game in there before they knocked it down. I have supported the club for around 30 years and I have always loved night games in the East End. The air used to be thick with smoke and the atmosphere was always good on a night game under floodlights. The end has changed over the years and to a certain extent so have the fans who go in that area. But that night it was like a reunion. I saw loads of blokes I used to see when we stood on the terracing. It was a fantastic send off.

Ray Gower
Brislington

Printed in Great Britain
by Amazon.co.uk, Ltd.,
Marston Gate.